HOPKINS: THEOLOGIAN'S POET

Introduction and a Commentary
on Selected Poems

HOPKINS: THEOLOGIAN'S POET

Introduction and a Commentary on Selected Poems

AIDAN NICHOLS, OP

Sapientia Press
of Ave Maria University

Sapientia Press
of Ave Maria University
24 Frank Lloyd Wright Drive
Ann Arbor, MI 48106
888-343-8607

Cover Design: Eloise Anagnost

Printed in the United States of America.

Library of Congress Control Number: 2006921773

ISBN-10: 1-932589-29-5

ISBN-13: 978-1-932589-29-0

*At the core of Hopkins' 'theopoetics' is the assumption
that all words are seeking to rejoin and to recall the
ultimate Word which is their source.*

—JUSTUS GEORGE LAWLER

*To draw all things back to Christ, as a crossbow strains
to propel its arrow, the poet inscaped and worded
what he saw and understood.*

—JAMES FINN COTTER

*The fact that all natures and selves are fashioned and
determined for Christ, who is both their ultimate inscape
and instress, means that there is no other possibility
of reading them objectively than in relation to this centre
in which they are integrated.*

—HANS URS VON BALTHASAR

TABLE OF CONTENTS

THIS BOOK is not intended for professional Hopkins scholars, who, should they ever see it, will probably find it a curious and unsatisfactory mixture of genres. They will not object much to the Introduction, which had the advantage of the two superb biographies of Hopkins that appeared almost simultaneously at the start of the 1990s. But in the Commentary, though I make use of some of the findings of literary criticism, I allow myself free rein to go beyond its scholarly limits.

The aim is to offer not only a reading of Hopkins's poems —necessarily modest, for reasons both of space and of the author's limitations. Beyond this, I set out some theological reflections stimulated by the poems and congruent with them though not demonstrably demanded by them—even in that weak sense of "demonstrably", which the study of such unusual poetry can bear. Hopkins was a self-consciously orthodox Catholic, and it is hard to see how placing his poems within a setting of theological doctrine can be said to reduce, rather than enhance, understanding.

My purpose has been to commend Hopkins and his work to new readers, and especially to his fellow-religionists among them, by indicating the wider theological bearings of his poems. If my words will encourage some of these to enter into the unique world, at once mysterious and precise, Hopkins opens up, I shall consider I have achieved my aim.

The poems I have chosen are arranged in their chrono-logical order of composition, with one exception. Taking the advice of the great Hopkins commentator (and editor)

Norman MacKenzie, I have placed "The Wreck of the Deutschland"—the longest and most demanding of these poems, but also the earliest—at the end.

—AIDAN NICHOLS, OP
Blackfriars, Cambridge
Feast of the Blessed Virgin Mary of the Rosary
2005

INTRODUCTION

. . .

Hopkins's Early Upbringing

GERARD HOPKINS (he rarely used his middle name, Manley) was born on 28 July 1844 in the Essex village of Stratford.[1] His birthplace, "Chestnut House", 87 The Grove, can no longer be a place of pilgrimage, since it was destroyed during Hitler's war, in the bombing raids of 1941. At the time of Hopkins's boyhood, the fringes of the Essex countryside were rapidly losing, through creeping industrialisation, whatever charm they had once possessed. So the Hopkins family, which was well-to-do middle class, decided to move to the decidedly fashionable, and leafy, district of Hampstead, which is still, by reputation, London's most literary quarter. Gerard was the eldest son of Manley Hopkins, a marine insurance adjuster, whose knowledge of the ocean and penchant for poetry—his mildly competent verse appeared in contemporary anthologies alongside Christina Rossetti's[2]—influenced the mind and sensibility of the growing boy. So did his devout, if moderate, High Anglican churchmanship: warned against the local vicar as "very low", the children suspected him of dastardly crimes![3] Kate Hopkins, Gerard's mother,

---

[1] The two principal biographies, both richly documented, are: R. B. Martin, *Gerard Manley Hopkins. A Very Private Life* (London 1991), and N. White, *Hopkins. A Literary Biography* (London 1993). The former, which is exquisitely written, rather overdoes an attempt at psychosexual analysis. For a shot across the author's bows, see J. G. Lawler, *Hopkins Re-constructed. Life, Poetry and the Tradition* (New York 1998), 47–94.

[2] N. White, *Hopkins. A Literary Biography* (Oxford 1992), 6.

[3] Ibid., 17.

knew German, which was rapidly acquiring the status of the most prestigious language for literature and philosophy. She was interested in music, poetry, and the visual arts. Victorian gentlewomen were habituated to sketching, but it seems worth noting that her kin, who were Smiths, were related by marriage to Thomas Gainsborough, one of the first English artists to paint not idealised classical landscapes but the actual scenes of his native land. This was, then, a creative family. Perhaps their single most precious gift to Gerard was the delight in verbal dexterity that sparkled in their love of puns.

Gerard shared—up to a point—the painterly gifts of his brothers Arthur and Everard, both of whom became professional artists.[4] John Ruskin, at the height of his influence in England, was their chosen model, both in the techniques of his drawings, with their close observations of natural forms, and in his glowing word-paintings of nature. "A comparison between their diaries shows the huge degree to which Ruskin influenced Hopkins."[5] Ruskin hoped to capture in words the exact observation, combined with a sense of nature's elemental forms, relations, and energy, which he divined in the canvases of J. M. W. Turner. Hopkins's familiarity with Ruskin's advocacy of Turner in *Modern Painters*, as well as his Anglican Christianity, disposed him to share Ruskin's conviction that nature carries the creative imprint of God.

At Highgate Grammar School (strictly, "Sir Roger Cholmeley's School"), it was, however, Hopkins's poetic

---

[4] For reproductions of his artistic work, and that of his brothers and the better known artists in whom he showed interest—not only Ruskin but also the Pre-Raphaelites, as well as contemporary photographs of sites pertinent to his life and work, see R. K. R. Thornton (ed.), *All My Eyes See. The Visual World of Gerard Manley Hopkins* (Sunderland 1975).

[5] N. White, "The Context of Hopkins' Drawings", in ibid., 53–67, and here at 64.

gifts and his flair for the classics that were chiefly encouraged. His earliest poems are rather in the idiom of John
Keats, soft, luscious, and highly decorated, altogether unlike
his tense mature verse—though even that has its Keatsian
moments. At school he rebelled against an evangelical mar-
tinet of a headmaster. Along with his humour, that quelled
any murmurings on the part of his peers that his academic
achievements might otherwise have prompted. In fact, his
school did him proud. The quality of tuition offered, combined with the native talents of the pupil, enabled him to
gain not only a place but a subsidised "Exhibition" (albeit at
the second attempt) at Balliol College, Oxford, where he
studied from 1863 to 1867. At this time, Balliol was entering its golden age as Oxford's intellectual acme. It was a college that encouraged not simply scholars but what S. T.
Coleridge would have called a "clerisy"—learned men with
leading ideas for civil society. Its fellowship constituted
something of an "intelligentsia" in the Continental European sense. They eschewed the customary Oxbridge toler-
ance of slackers. Hopkins would be expected to work.

. . .

Hopkins at Oxford

At Oxford Hopkins read *Literae humaniores*, popularly
known from its final examination as "Greats". This faculty
furnished a traditional education, based on philosophy,
along with ancient history and literature. Linguistic skills
were honed, but the course chiefly emphasised the development of analytical and critical faculties in the handling of
both texts and ideas. By the 1860s Oxford was increasingly
examination-oriented, a consequence of the British State's
increasing need for competent future administrators. A

number of Hopkins's undergraduate essays survive, and allow us to detect even so early a sophisticated and confident intelligence at work. "Classics" as then defined was tough-minded (the syllabus contained little in the way of lyric or pastoral poetry). At a time when the arts, including theology, and sciences were not so separate as they later became—during Hopkins's student days, clergymen made up a considerable proportion of the membership of the British Association for the Advancement of Science—candidates were encouraged to take into account not only early modern and modern philosophy but developments in the natural sciences too.[6] "Philosophy" was deemed to cover the history of science and scientific method or methods considered categories of logic.

Like many educated Victorians, Hopkins would become something of an amateur scientist, as his contributions to the flagship journal of British science, *Nature*, suffice to show. In his letters to the editor and reports for *Nature*'s readers, "science" here was not so different, however, from eighteenth-century natural history, the description of species in their habitats or of astronomical phenomena in the night sky. Hopkins would have been exposed at Oxford (and afterward) to more troublesome issues, whether in the life sciences, as with Charles Darwin's 1859 study *The Origin of Species*, or in the physical sciences, through the contemporary revival of the atomism of ancient philosophers such as Lucretius.

Hopkins's surviving essays show, it is said, a combination of Platonic idealism and Aristotelian realism. This is approx-

---

6 The university reforms of the 1850s had created a new "school" (faculty) of natural science, as well as one of law and history. It could not compete with the prestige of Greats and attracted-comparatively few students. For the background, see T. Zaniello, *Hopkins in the Age of Darwin* (Iowa City 1988), 11–34.

imately what we might expect given his teachers: notably
Benjamin Jowett, the Master of Balliol, a liberal Christian
Platonist, T. H. Green, an opponent of empiricism, and Wal-
ter Pater, an eclectic—but mainly Epicurean—aesthetician.
The undergraduate Hopkins evinced especial aptitude for
questions of perception, and demonstrated a conviction that
if we would have an adequate philosophy of mind, we must
posit, beyond the dance of atoms, a world of order.

> He was groping for a theory of perception that would
> involve the mind's active participation in the perception of
> nature. Science 'without metaphysics', as he wrote, was
> 'scopeless', 'atomic', that is, incoherent and without direc-
> tion. . . . [W]ithout the mind's active participation in the
> discovery of special forms in nature and without the recog-
> nition that God's creative power sustained those forms—in
> brief, without inscape and instress—the atomist random-
> ness of natural events, the anti-metaphysician's dream,
> would prevail.[7]

But this was not the only spiritual front on which the student Hopkins was battling. Even without his Anglican home
background he would have had to come to terms with academic Christianity in some way: an examination in Divinity
was compulsory for all students before graduation. As things
turned out, despite Balliol's reputation for "Broad Church"
or Latitudinarian Christianity unfussed about doctrine or
Church tradition, Oxford was also where Hopkins discovered, in a far fuller form than parental religion provided, the
High Church Anglicanism of the Tractarian Revival. One of
the giants of that movement, E. B. Pusey, Regius Professor of
Hebrew at Christ Church, still lived. But owing to Pusey's

---

[7] Ibid., 56–57.

reclusiveness as well as advancing years, the flame of the "Oxford Movement" was passing to men of a younger generation, and notably the doctrinal theologian and celebrated preacher Henry Liddon, whom Hopkins took as a father confessor. Anglo-Catholicism—into which Tractarianism was gradually mutating, thanks to the injection of hormones from Tridentine Roman Catholicism—attracted Hopkins not so much for its aesthetic qualities as for its Eucharistic, devotional, and (in some cases) ascetical intensity. It gave him for the first time the idea of Christian celibacy.

Without surrendering all this baggage, he eventually found the Anglo-Catholic position an unstable halfway house to Rome. His first Catholic hero appears to have been the fifteenth-century Florentine Dominican Girolamo Savonarola, who combined high morals and primitive monastic observance with remarkable fluency in writing and, it might be added, an ambivalent attitude to the arts (Christian, yes; pagan, no). Though Hopkins knew Villari's life of Savonarola, it was George Eliot's fictionalised study, *Romola,* which really enthused him. But one does not enter ecclesial communion through books. Hopkins's way to the Church was through John Henry Newman "of the Oratory"—and specifically of the Oratory of the sprawling manufacturing and commercial city of Birmingham, the centre, under the restored Roman hierarchy in England, of the diocese where Oxford was situated. Newman was at the height of his fame, his *Apologia pro vita sua*—one of the great texts of Victorian high culture—having appeared in 1864. He treated the final year undergraduate with a well-conceived combination of gravity and lightness. In the end, Hopkins's conversion to Rome was neither literary nor based on hero worship. Rather, it was argumentative. Here alone was authoritative revelational Christianity with an apologetic that did not leak.

To parental dismay, on 21 October 1866 Newman received Hopkins into the Roman Catholic Church. Manley Hopkins appealed to Liddon for help in saving his son from what he termed, rather brutally but not altogether unfairly:

> throwing a pure life and a somewhat unusual intellect away in the cold limbo which Rome assigns her English converts.[8]

Hopkins fils seems rather to have relished the situation, as is clear from his letters of the period, which, it has been said, "reveal a characteristic blend of integrity and stubborn legalistic obstinacy".[9] This did not prevent Newman from accepting him as a teacher at the Oratory School, an appointment which was certainly merited by his academic triumph—a "Double First"—in the Oxford "Schools", or Final Examinations. It was not an especially agreeable experience—R. B. Martin amusingly compares its inconveniences to the "misery of masters and boys" at "Llanabba Castle" in Evelyn Waugh's comic novel *Decline and Fall*.[10] But for the student of his intellectual temper it is not without importance. From it dates the jotted notes on the pre-Socratic philosopher Parmenides where he uses for the first time two key terms for the plotting of that temper— "inscape" and "instress", and does so, as Norman White remarks, "with a sense of familiarity and confidence".[11]

> All things are upheld by instress, and are meaningless without it. [Parmenides'] feeling for instress, for the flush and foredrawn, and for inscape is most striking and from this

8 *Further Letters of Gerard Manley Hopkins*, ed. C. C. Abbott (London 1956, 2nd edition), 435. Cited below as Further Letters.
9 D. McChesney, *A Hopkins Commentary. An Explanatory Commentary on the Main Poems, 1876–1889* (London 1968), 5.
10 R. B. Martin, *Gerard Manley Hopkins*, 167–68.
11 N. White, *Hopkins*, 158.

one can understand Plato's reverence for him as the great
father of Realism. . . . [I]ndeed I have often felt the depth
of an instress or how fast the inscape holds a thing that
nothing is so pregnant and straightforward to the truth as
simple *yes* and *is*.[12]

Meanwhile he was marking time before entering the
novitiate of the Society of Jesus, then one of Catholicism's
most rigorous orders. This, no doubt, is what attracted
Hopkins to it—as well as its reputation as the crack troops
of the Roman Church. He admired action men.

Hopkins celebrated his own *vita nuova* by a walking tour
in the Swiss Alps, of which he has left a vigorous account in
his *Journals*. He was aware that this was his last chance to
sample that magnificent Victorian playground of strenuous
exercise and conversation: by federal law, no Jesuit was per-
mitted to enter Switzerland, where the dominant cantons
were strongly Protestant in character. Hopkins also took the
opportunity to burn some of his early poetry, which he evidently deemed incongruous with a sacerdotal vocation of an
ascetic stamp. Prudently, he sent copies of some of the better ones to his university friend Robert Bridges for safekeep-
ing. He wrote no further poetry worth mentioning until
1875, when, to the mystification of his Jesuit confreres, and
on the vaguest of hints from a superior, he produced "The
Wreck of the Deutschland", which Bridges somewhat
harshly called a "dragon" turning potential readers from the
gates. Though alarmed by the innovative character of Hopkins's poems, and their apparent difficulty, Bridges would

---

12 *The Journals and Papers of Gerard Manley Hopkins*, ed. H. House,
    completed by G. Storey (London 1959), 127. Cited below as
    Journals. It should be said that this is a somewhat maverick read-
    ing of the Parmenidean fragments which figure here more as what
    the Germans call a *Hilfsmittel* for the emergence of Hopkins's own
    ontological insight.

become his literary executor and, thirty years after his death, release his poetry on a startled world.

. . .

Hopkins and the English Jesuits

THE ENGLISH PROVINCE of the Society of Jesus was one of its oldest and most distinguished—famous for missionaries and martyrs, poets and schoolmasters, and, in general, highly trained and professionally minded priests.[13] Showing the typical phlegm of the island race, the superiors of the English Province paid as little attention as possible to the bull *Dominus ac Redemptor* suppressing the Jesuits—largely at the behest of their opponents in the political elites of France, Portugal, and Spain—in 1773. Only the Revolutionary wars catalysed by tumultuous events in Paris drove them from their college in Flanders to the comparative safety of an England where anti-Jacobinism had become more serious a passion than anti-popery. They retreated to an enormous Elizabethan house in the Ribble Valley of central Lancashire: Stonyhurst, where Hopkins would do his Catholic, as distinct from Oxford, study of philosophy. (The Jesuit ordinands, however, lived in a more recently constructed barracks-like building, later dignified by the name of St Mary's Hall.) On the formal restoration of the Society by Pius VII in 1814 neither the British Government nor the English Catholic bishops proved wildly enthusiastic. Owing to a certain nervousness about public opinion, English Jesuit novices long made their vows privately. The Catholic Emancipation Act had included a clause excluding the Jesuits from its permissive provisions,

---

[13] F. Edwards, SJ, *The Jesuits in England from 1589 to the Present Day* (Tunbridge Wells 1993).

though in practice this was a dead letter. By Hopkins's time the "novitiate"—a "desert period" of initiation into the Society's way of life and ethos—was done at Bessborough House overlooking Richmond Park, once a favoured venue of the Prince Regent but renamed "Manresa" after the hermitage of the Jesuits' founder, Ignatius Loyola. Certain changes involving more than nomenclature were made. With a philistinism which unfortunately marred the restored Society, so one of Hopkins's biographers complains, the Jesuit superiors "set about the familiar process of guaranteeing sanctity by the systematic destruction of beauty".[14] Hopkins's sense of beauty was hardly conventional, however, and he may not have regretted the mansion's missing chandeliers.

Not till mid-century did the English Province enjoy an upsurge of vocations. A sign of the increased numbers of recruits was the opening of a separate theologate, St Beuno's, in the Clwyd Valley of North Wales. There Hopkins's happiest years as a Jesuit were spent, and his most loved nature poems written.

Possibly Hopkins was atypical of his brethren. Until the Great War of 1914–18, long after Hopkins's death, intellectuals could not be called numerous, whereas scions of the landed classes were. A characteristic "brief life" of the recusant Jesuits lent itself readily to satire:

> He completed his studies at Ghent
> And most likely to England was sent.
> Of his death there's no trace,
> As to time or to place.
> He was Scotch and of noble descent.[15]

---

[14] R. B. Martin, *Gerard Manley Hopkins*, 184.

[15] Cited in M. Walsh, "The Jesuits of England", *The Tablet* 26 (July 2003): 12.

In another sense, however, Hopkins was typical. He typified the intake of Oxonian Puseyites "crossing the Tiber". This would create certain difficulties, granted the need of the Province to staff not only its colleges but also its parishes, often located in the terrible—and, as to Catholicism, largely Irish-dominated—Industrial Revolution towns.

. . .

Hopkins at Stonyhurst

FROM THE STANDPOINT of his poetic development, Hopkins's novitiate might not seem to have been especially significant, though the bucolic loveliness of Richmond Park, which once inspired Turner, can hardly have failed to make an impression. But for the life from which the poetry is inseparable, the role of the aspirations he formed there can hardly be overestimated. He approached his vocation in a sacrificial, oblatory frame of mind.[16] As he wrote later, in correspondence:

> This I say: my vocation puts before me a standard so high that a higher can be found nowhere else. The question then for me is not whether I am willing . . . to make a sacrifice of hopes of fame . . . but whether I am not to undergo a severe judgment from God for the lothness I have shown in making it . . . for the backward glances I have given with my hand on the plough.[17]

Sacrificium intellectus—the renunciation of thought— did not enter this, as his years in the Jesuit philosophate at

---

[16] Let us hope that the regimen and ethos, if fairly represented by the account assembled in N. White, *Hopkins,* 172–87, was lightened at least occasionally by a sense of humour.

[17] *Correspondence of Gerard Manley Hopkins and R. W. Dixon,* ed. C. C. Abbott (London 1956, 2nd edition), 88.

Stonyhurst would demonstrate. It was natural that Stonyhurst—as close as the English Jesuits got to a "mother
house"—should stimulate the historical imagination. The
Arundell Library and various permanent exhibitions dis-
played not only pre-Reformation illuminated manuscripts
and incunabula but artefacts redolent of the entire history
of the post-Reformation Catholicism in Britain: a first edition of the *Defence of the Seven Sacraments,* for which Pope
Leo X had declared Henry VIII "Defender of the Faith";
books and pamphlets from secret recusant presses; Stuart
and Jacobite memorabilia.[18] But more than this, Hopkins
formed part of a group of intellectually ambitious Stonyhurst Jesuits who sought to apply scholastic thought to contemporary anti-sceptical purposes. His scientific interests
were stimulated by the—nationally renowned—Stonyhurst
observatory cum meteorological station, and he redoubled
his practice of close observation of nature. The wildness of
the Lancashire countryside—Pendle Hill of witches' fame,
the peat-stained rivers, and the bare moorland—galvanised
the descriptions he recorded in his journals, which now
acquire that potently tactile quality associated with his
poetry and prose. Long before he resumed the serious writing of poetry, Hopkins was noting how, in receptive observation at its most engaged, there seems to be a curious
intercommunication of mind and thing, self and other.
Then through a chance find in Stonyhurst's library, he discovered the late-thirteenth-century metaphysician John
Duns Scotus, whose philosophy of individual form chimed
with his own insights into the distinctive patterning
("inscape") and energy ("instress") of beings. He recorded
in his journals:

---

18 A. Hewitson, *Stonyhurst College, Its Past and Present* (Preston
1878, 2nd edition).

At this time I had first begun to get hold of the copy of Scotus on the Sentences in the Baddely library and was flushed with a new stroke of enthusiasm. It may come to nothing or it may be a mercy from God. But just then when I took in any inscape of the sky or sea I thought of Scotus.[19]

Scotism certainly confirmed Hopkins in his ardour for particular form. To what extent the metaphysics, doctrine, and devotion of his *poetry* is indebted to Scotus, rather than to the wider Latin Catholic tradition and its classical interpretative forms, is something that can be disputed. Much in the ontological underpinnings of his verse could also be expressed in terms drawn from the chief master of his Jesuit education, Thomas Aquinas. His sermons, where Hopkins was orating in expository and explanatory mode, are a different matter.

When in 1872–73 Hopkins taught budding Jesuits "rhetoric"—an introduction to literature and logic—at Manresa House, he started to work out his peculiar ideas on metre and rhythm as well as to apply his theory of inscape to poetry.[20] Hopkins distinguished common or "running" rhythm, where in the structure of verse the feet tend to be regular—based on a strict counting of syllables— from "sprung" rhythm, where this is emphatically not the case. As his modern editor, Norman H. MacKenzie, felicitously remarks:

---

[19] *Journals,* 221. The "Sentences" were Peter Lombard's high mediaeval compendium of theology, used as a textbook in the schools down to the sixteenth century. All the great scholastics of the Middle Ages left commentaries on it. "The Baddely (*recte* Badeley) library" was a collection donated by Edward Badeley, a friend of Newman's.

[20] *Journals,* 267–90.

The name suggests the natural grace of a deer springing
down a mountainside, adjusting the length of each leap
according to the ground it is covering.[21]

Hopkins himself put it like this to Bridges:

> Why do I employ sprung rhythm at all? Because it is the
> nearest to the rhythm of prose, that is the native and natu-
> ral rhythm of speech, the least forced, the most rhetorical
> and emphatic of all possible rhythms, combining, as it
> seems to me, opposite and, one wd. have thought, incom-
> patible excellences, markedness of rhythm—that is
> rhythm's self—and naturalness of expression.[22]

And about the importance of the concept of "inscape" to
Hopkins's poetic art there can be little doubt. He would
later write to his friend Robert Bridges:

> But as air, melody, is what strikes me most of all in music and
> design in painting, so design, pattern or what I am in the
> habit of calling 'inscape' is what I above all aim at in poetry.[23]

A twentieth-century Jesuit commentator explains the subjacent ontology. Inscape is the unified complex of those sen-
suous qualities of some perceptual object which strike us as
at once integral to it and typical of it—and which thus
grant us unique insight into its essence. More than the
scholastic term *species*, of which Hopkins's own rendering

---

[21] N. H. MacKenzie, *A Reader's Guide to Gerard Manley Hopkins*
(London 1981), 238. MacKenzie notes, ibid., 239, that Hopkins's later poems indeed show a falling version of such rhythm
(consonant with MacKenzie's own deer metaphor), the early
ones a rising rhythm (from unstressed syllables to stressed).

[22] *The Letters of Gerard Manley Hopkins to Robert Bridges,* ed. C. C.
Abbott (London 1955, 2nd edition), 46. Cited below as *Letters.*

[23] Ibid., 66.

was "scape", it emphasises "the outward reflection of the *inner* nature of a thing" (hence *in*-scape). Unlike the medieval ontologists, Hopkins extended the scope of this vocabulary to a wider realm than natural kinds.

> Provided that in the poet's artistic vision the object of art shows forth an intrinsic unity that extends further than a mere harmonious ordering of parts as designated by pattern, the poet will grasp its inscape. Hence not only an organic being, as a flower, tree or animal, each a *unum per se*, will present itself to Hopkins's vision as an individual, but also objects of art, and even nature-scenes, can in his perception display a marked individuality.[24]

Only this justifies his remarks to Bridges. Actually, one could go further and say Hopkins found inscape in language itself, and in particular words.

In natural things, the power that sustains inscape Hopkins would call in time "instress".[25] Unlike inscape, instress is not perceived in itself but only in its effects. It is the energy or "stress" of being by which things are upheld and strive for continued existence. Evidently, in this context both inscape and instress are theologically pertinent. They express respectively the creative word and the preserving power of God. This explains Hopkins's "sacramental" view of nature. Creation is the "visible sign of an invisible, intelligent and creative energy".[26]

---

[24] W. A. M. Peters, SJ, *Gerard Manley Hopkins. A Critical Essay towards the Understanding of His Poetry* (London 1948; Oxford and New York 1971), 3.

[25] See L. Cochran, OP, in *Hopkins Quarterly* 6. 4 (1980): 143–81.

[26] D. McChesney, *A Hopkins Commentary*, 29.

· · ·
Hopkins in Wales

THE THREE YEARS Hopkins spent at St Beuno's, in lyri-
cally beautiful countryside, were surely the most serene of
his life. He wrote to his father, with whom full relations
had been restored:

> The house stands on a steep hillside, it commands the
> long-drawn valley of Clwyd to the sea, a vast prospect, and
> opposite is Snowdon and its range, just now it being bright
> visible but coming and going with the weather. The air
> seems to me very fresh and wholesome.[27]

So also was the atmosphere of his life. These years were crucial for his poetic output. He was already convinced of the
importance of the Anglo-Saxon roots of the English language, shunning, by and large, the Latinate contributions
of the Anglo-Norman nobility and later importations.
Now, however, he taught himself Welsh, and to the influence of Anglo-Saxon poetry was added the pervasive Welsh
poetic device of multiple alliteration and internal rhyming
(cynghanedd).[28] He remembered that his own father's
ancestors were Welsh and began to feel a "yearning" for the
Welsh people, regretting that so few of them were
Catholics. "St Winefred's Well", a medieval shrine that had
survived, more or less, the Reformation and the dwindling
of Welsh recusancy, was the goal of regular pilgrimages. It

---

[27] *Further Letters*, 124.
[28] It is impressive, if slightly alarming, to discover that the fullest
study of the influence of Welsh on Hopkins's poetry is in German: C. Küper, *Walisische Traditionen in der Dichtung von G. M.
Hopkins* (Bonn 1973).

was only a few miles from St Beuno's, and Hopkins loved strenuous walking. The combination of antiquity, martyrdom, and the possibility of miracle with *water*, his favourite element, proved irresistible.

Water, however, is an ambiguous medium. During these years—in December 1875, in fact—Hopkins was deeply moved by news of the wreck, off the English coast, of a German vessel bound for the United States, whither it was taking, among others, religious sisters expelled from their homeland as a consequence of the anti-Catholic legislation of the Prussian government under Count Bismarck. The editor of the Jesuit periodical *The Month* could make nothing of Hopkins's extraordinary diction and practice of rhythm in verse, though a more conventional poem, saluting the silver jubilee of the first Catholic bishop of Shrewsbury, proved more acceptable. (At this time the counties of North Wales were comprised within that diocese.) "The Wreck of the Deutschland" remains one of Hopkins's sublimest achievements. Of "The Silver Jubilee" we can best say it has its place through underlining the way Hopkins now felt free to continue to write poetry—even if for most of his lifetime its only readers were Bridges and an old school acquaintance, R. W. Dixon, an Anglican clergyman: not the worst audience he could have chosen inasmuch as both men were practising poets whose sincerity and humanity Hopkins admired. Sometimes overlooked, however, and certainly beyond the evaluative powers of Bridges and Dixon, is the congratulatory *cywydd*—a distinctive kind of alliterative verse—which he wrote at the same time as a further offering to Bishop Brown. Here, even in translation, his love of Wales, its ancient Church and living landscapes, comes shining through as he invokes the divine blessing and supplicates God for the conversion of the Welsh: "Father, from thy hand will issue a spring from which will flow the beautiful prime good".[29]

These achievements did not, though, signify scholastic merit in the Jesuits' highly formal educational system. Hopkins did not do especially well in the theological examinations at St Beuno's. When he was rejected for a further year of study—probably the first time in his life he had disappointed the examiners—it rapidly became clear that he would not be a "high-flyer" in the Jesuit Province. But Trojans were needed for all kinds of work.

. . .

Hopkins and the Pastorate

Hopkins's ordination to the priesthood in September 1877 was followed by a number of assignments as pastor, preacher, schoolmaster, whether at Mount St Mary's, near Sheffield in Yorkshire (1877–78) or back at Stonyhurst; at The Immaculate Conception, Farm Street, in the prestigious London district of Mayfair (both in 1878), or in Oxford, where the Jesuits had a parish (1878–79); at the south Lancashire township of Bedford Leigh, near Manchester (1879), or in slum parishes in Liverpool and Glasgow (1880–81). All of these involved major disappointments as he sensed the disparity between his efforts and the expectations of others— whether parishioners or his colleagues. (A celebrated example is the Farm Street sermon where he regaled Mayfair ladies with a comparison of the Church's sacraments to the teats of a cow's udder.) The exception, curiously, was in Lancashire— excluding Liverpool, which, as the port-of-entry of the Irish poor and a byword for mass industrial degradation, was

---

[29] Cited in N. White, *Hopkins,* 263. The full text can be found in C. Phillips (ed.), *Gerard Manley Hopkins* (Oxford 1986), 344–45.

another matter. At Leigh he found the people resilient, happy, and responsive.

> Our flock are fervent, I have not seen their equal. . . . Oxford was not to me a congenial place, I am far more at home with the Lancashire people.[30]

At Oxford he was in an odd position, alienated by Catholicism, priesthood, and Jesuitry from those culturally closest to him—in contrast to the domestic servants and navvies at St Aloysius, or the shopkeepers and boardinghouse landladies who far exceeded dons and undergraduates as converts there. He reacted by describing the university itself in hostile terms: it was "alien", "chilling", "deeply to be distrusted".[31] How, then, could he have been at ease in the university-dominated town? Nowhere, however, was as deeply depressing to him as Liverpool, where the sordid scenes he witnessed drew from him an early confession of that profound weariness and malaise which would later best him in Dublin: "Human nature is so inveterate. . . . Would that I had seen the last of it".[32]

During this period, the English Jesuits were hard-pressed for manpower. But it is scarcely a good sign that none of Hopkins's assignations lasted over a year. Nonetheless, all these postings were marked by poetic work (including several of the finest of his poems). They also occasioned, naturally enough, the writing of his sermons, where passages of considerable directness vie with the Baroque.

---

[30] *Further Letters*, 243.
[31] Ibid., 244.
[32] *Letters*, 110.

· · ·

Hopkins and Academe

FROM 1881 TO 1882 Hopkins fulfilled the require-
ments of the "Tertianship", a sort of second novitiate for
Jesuits in midlife. The notes he wrote then on Ignatian
Exercises have been regarded as illuminating not only for his
spirituality but for his poetry too. In the late summer of
1882, he returned for the last time to Stonyhurst with a
commission to prepare for university the high-flying classi-
cists among the school's cream of students. (His stay was
notable for the intense correspondence he initiated with an
"established" Victorian poet, Coventry Patmore.) This was,
in retrospect, a preamble to the post he received in 1884,
when he became professor of Greek and Latin literature at
University College, Dublin—the institution founded by
Newman as the "Catholic University College" but newly
acquired by the Jesuits from the Irish hierarchy, who considered it a white elephant. At the same time he was made a
fellow in classics in the Royal University of Ireland—as its
name suggests, a national body which had campuses in
Belfast, Galway, and Cork, as well as a constitutional connexion to the college in Dublin.

Unfortunately, the tedious slog of examining (a considerable part of his duties under the latter rubric, and the
scripts were numbered annually not so much in hundreds
as in thousands), combined with the homesickness and
sense of alienation he felt in Ireland to undermine his mental peace. These were years of nationalist agitation, and
Hopkins, whose English patriotism was passionate, felt iso-
lated and wrong-footed by his new colleagues. He acknowledged the historic grievances of the Catholic Irish, but not
the rightness of the solution proposed: dissolution of the
bond with Britain and the empire. In the notes of his last

retreat, after acknowledging what was positive about his
work, he went on:

> Meanwhile the Catholic Church in Ireland and the Irish
> Province in it and our College in that are greatly given over
> to a partly unlawful cause, promoted by partly unlawful
> means, and against my will my pains, laborious and dis-
> tasteful, like prisoners made to serve the enemies' gunners,
> go to help on this cause.[33]

Not that all of the Irish parties involved wanted his help.
The provincial of the Irish Province disapproved in principle of English converts working in Ireland, and in Hopkins's case, through inverted intellectual snobbery, the
president of Maynooth and the Archbishop of Dublin
agreed. His appointment "was a lasting grievance to the
defeated faction".[34] Moreover, the students to whom Hopkins delivered his over-prepared lectures were unreceptive
and sometimes boorish, the library facilities quite inadequate. Above all, his persona—and therefore, it seemed, his
person—was out of place.

> Many of his characteristics—appearance, way of talking,
> Newmanite conversion, shyness and reclusiveness, edu-
> cated upper-class English and Oxonian mannerisms,
> scrupulous habits, interests in music and the visual arts,
> poetic compositions—appeared typical facets of an English
> aesthete. . . . He could be understood in Dublin only as an
> example of English aesthetic Catholicism, with which the
> Irish had no sympathy.[35]

---

[33] Cited from the papers of Robert Bridges, as deposited in Bodley's
Library at Oxford, in R. B. Martin, *Gerard Manley Hopkins,* 409.

[34] N. White, *Hopkins,* 357.

[35] Ibid., 382, 383.

In these unpropitious circumstances, the various demons he had faced down—or at any rate faced—in the course of his short life now took up their abode. Deeper than the rational complaints there was a well of dreadful and— humanly speaking—unassuageable loneliness. The "Dark" or "Terrible" Sonnets are the upshot. He wrote to Bridges:

> All impulse fails me: I can give myself no sufficient reason for going on. Nothing comes: I am a eunuch—but it is for the kingdom of heaven's sake.[36]

But though Hopkins's Dublin period was in one sense a disaster, inducing melancholia and depression, he also knew periods of buoyancy, usually coinciding with spells in the Ireland of the countryside and the coast, or holidays in the rest of the British Isles. Not all the poetry of these years is a poetry of desolation. At the same time, the poems written under the impact of his negative experiences are superb testimonies to the human spirit in its capacity to endure.

In early May 1889 Hopkins fell ill with fever. He seemed to be mending but during the night of 5 June took a turn for the worse. His parents were called, and on the morning of 8 June 1889 he received the last rites. He died that day. Hopkins was buried in the plot owned by the Jesuits in Dublin's Glasnevin Cemetery. The sanitary arrangements at 86 St Stephen's Green had left much to be desired. The typhoid fever to which he succumbed was not a specialty of the city on the Liffey, dirty as it was, but a periodic danger in any conurbation of Victorian Britain.

---

[36] *Letters,* 270.

. . .

Hopkins and Posterity

B Y AND LARGE, Robert Bridges served Hopkins well as his literary executor.[37] To keep his memory alive, he arranged for the publication of some few poems, by way of a memoir, more or less straight away. This fell resoundingly flat. So he waited until he judged the literary climate propitious for the release of the complete oeuvre. In his wartime anthology *The Spirit of Man* he ventured to include half a dozen complete poems and some parts of others. This time the response was different. Given Bridges's standing as poet laureate from 1913 until his death in 1930, his advocacy was already a major point in Hopkins's favour. But that was by no means the whole story. In September 1917 he wrote to Hopkins's mother:

> I have had lately some very authoritative appeals for the publication of all Gerard's poetical remains. The 'Spirit of Man' has had a wide sale, and his poems in it have commanded a good deal of attention. The other day Sir Walter Raleigh, [professor of English literature at Oxford] whose judgment is very highly esteemed, said to me that Gerard's poems in The Spirit of Man were the only ones among the comparatively unknown writers whom I had introduced, which stood up alongside of the greater writers. And this

---

[37] However, Bridges's public apology for the ungrammatical quality of Hopkins's language, though doubtless designed to forestall criticism, sent many critics down the wrong track. Inspired by his study of dialect and philology, Hopkins's poetic "heightening" of current language was an intensification of the force not of standard prose but of common—and especially of rural—speech: thus J. Milroy, *The Language of Gerard Manley Hopkins* (London 1977), 2–32, and passim. For Victorian word-collectors, rural speech had preserved "older forms unsullied by standardization, bookishness and artificiality", ibid., 84.

afternoon I met a man who had just come from Petrograd, who said much the same thing. He was very urgent about having a complete edition.

And he added, "I think the time has come to publish all the poems".[38] The first edition of the poems appeared, accordingly, in 1918—with Hopkins's middle name, Manley, included on the title page owing to a worry about confusion with his nephew, also Gerard, by then a well-known translator. Ever since the second edition, dated to 1930, Hopkins's stock has continued to rise. Many would now rate him the outstanding English poet of the nineteenth century—a century of extraordinary literary flowering in our country. He and his work have been the object of some three thousand books and articles. One notes that among the most distinguished critics are his fellow Jesuits.

That process of reclamation began in 1920, when an unsigned group of Hopkins's confreres, writing simply as "Plures", contributed an important memoir to a commemorative issue of the then-premier British Catholic journal, *The Dublin Review*. Their judgment has been borne out by the best scholars since. As one of the latter sums up:

> The judgment of Plures amounts to this: Hopkins was 'an English mystic compounded of Benjamin Jowett and Duns Scotus', with an extraordinary talent for 'freakish' mirth and for searching out 'the odd and the whimsical'. He had nonetheless chosen a hard and unrewarding life as a Jesuit, fit neither by character nor by discipline to be one. . . . Plures argued that Hopkins' sensitive nature had been built upon Walter Pater's and John Ruskin's aestheticism, his philosophical views upon Jowett's Platonism, and his

---

[38] D. E. Stanford (ed.), *The Selected Letters of Robert Bridges* (London 1983), II., 725, cited N. White, *Hopkins*, 464.

Catholicism upon Cardinal Newman's doggedness. . . . The influence of Oxford had been crucial.[39]

In Plures's opinion, plainly, Hopkins could have said with Newman, it was not Catholics who made him a Catholic. It was Oxford that did so.

Gerard Hopkins entered into the Catholic Christian vision of creation and redemption with all the rich energies of his mind and heart. He also suffered acutely from a sense of the failure not simply of projects for books that never saw the light of day but also of the pastoral and educational charges he undertook in the Church's service. The latter were not burdens thrust upon him by the Jesuit Society in a spirit of making round pegs fit square holes. Within the—inevitably—limited range of possible assignments with which his superiors were faced, the difficulties he encountered were simply the way, for someone of his diffidence and sensitivity, things fell out. To a limited degree, the English Jesuits gave him a sense of belonging to a holy brotherhood. The Society of Jesus was a clerical organisation (though with "temporal coadjutors", lay brothers who did the domestic labour). It was not an order of monks or canons regular, consisting of stable communities each with a closely bonded conventual life. In any case, the personality traits which made Hopkins prey to recurring feelings of self-disillusionment and loneliness were well established before entry and would not have been easy to dislodge. In his meditation notes on the *Spiritual Exercises* he had written, "Let all consider this: we are our own tormentors".[40]

Hopkins's secular biographers have recorded a verdict of contradiction between the lives of priest and poet, or, more recently, the celibate and the man in love with human (espe-

---

[39] T. Zaniello, *Hopkins in the Age of Darwin,* 6.
[40] Cited N. White, *Hopkins,* 378.

cially male) beauty. Discounting the strata of the human personality where grace and nature—not without some tension—meet and embrace, they run the risk of counting for nothing, then, his dying words, "I am so happy, I am so happy".[41] Probably such critics have not weighed sufficiently an entry in his retreat notes for 1883, on the eve of his mission in Ireland:

> In meditating on the Crucifixion I saw how my asking to be raised to a higher degree of grace was asking also to be lifted on a higher cross. Then I took it that our Lord recommended me to our Lady and her to me.[42]

---

[41] Cited R. B. Martin, *Gerard Manley Hopkins,* 413.

[42] *The Sermons and Devotional Writings of Gerard Manley Hopkins,* ed. C. Devlin, SJ (Oxford 1967), 253–54. Cited below as *Sermons.*

POEMS & COMMENTARY

. . .

God's Grandeur

THE world is charged with the grandeur of God.
  It will flame out, like shining from shook foil;
  It gathers to a greatness, like the ooze of oil
Crushed. Why do men then now not reck his rod?
Generations have trod, have trod, have trod;
  And all is seared with trade; bleared, smeared with toil;
  And wears man's smudge and shares man's smell: the soil
Is bare now, nor can foot feel, being shod.

And for all this, nature is never spent;
  There lives the dearest freshness deep down things;
And though the last lights off the black West went
  Oh, morning, at the brown brink eastwards, springs—
Because the Holy Ghost over the bent
  World broods with warm breast and with ah! bright wings.

· · · · · · ·

This poem was written at St Beuno's, on 23 February 1877.
That the world is filled with God's glory is the firm conviction of the Church, issuing from a confluence of Scripture,
metaphysics, and the liturgy. The *Sanctus*, one of the most
ancient portions of the liturgies of East and West, declares
the heavens and the earth to be full of God's glory, thus
extending to all creation the cry the prophet Isaiah heard in
the Jerusalem temple during his call-vision in the year king
Uzziah died: "Holy, holy, holy, is the Lord of hosts; the
whole earth is full of his glory" (6:3). Hopkins, however,

prefers to the more customary "glory" the word "grandeur". The German language, as used in the title of his theological aesthetics by the Swiss dogmatician Hans Urs von Balthasar, throws light here. *Herrlichkeit* means not only "glory" but "lordliness": not just God's splendid radiance but his sovereign authority as well. Not for nothing does the Ambrosian hymn, the *Te Deum*, call what fills heaven and earth *majestatem gloriae tuae*, "the majesty of your glory". These interrelated divine attributes are well captured in Hopkins's word.

With this "grandeur" the world is "charged". The world is not only freighted with it, as in cargo carried aboard, though indeed God is present in all things simply through the way he causes their existence. More than this, though, the world is rendered by God a conduit for his wondrous self-streaming power. The recent (to Hopkins) invention of electricity intensifies the force of this opening statement of the sonnet. The divine glory surges through the world's circuit. God's grandeur, Hopkins goes on, "will flame out". From Sinai to Pentecost, the manifestation of God's glory has been experienced in and as fire. When the divine irrupts not merely naturally but supernaturally into our finite experience, the prophetic consciousness—in Moses on the mountain and during the wilderness wanderings, or as with the apostles in the Cenacle—registers God's action in flames of fire, the most striking and dramatic of the cosmic elements. But such theophanies—the burning bush, the fire-bursts on the mountain, the fiery pillar, and the tongues of fire at the first Whitsun—have their more modest correspondences in lesser epiphanies which may occur at any time. God's glory *will* flame out—that is its natural tendency, for all God's creative and salvific work attests his consistently communicative character—and it will do so "like shining from shook foil". We know from Hopkins's letters that in this comparison he was thinking, more specifically, of gold-foil, but doing so in a way that suggests the fire symbolism of revelation. Looked at from the side, gold-foil appears dull, as does the world to impercipient viewing. But when such foil is shaken, it

> gives off broad glares like sheet lightning and also, and this is true of nothing else, owing to its zigzag dints and creasings and network of many small cornered facets, a sort of fork lightning too.[43]

So we must know how to look at the world to see it aflame, and this is with what Augustine calls *fides oculata*, the "faith that has eyes". In his meditations Hopkins almost repeated the opening lines of this poem: "All things . . . are charged with God". But there he went on to insist—replacing his more usual focus on the sense of sight with an appeal to the sense of touch—that only "if we know how to touch them" will they "give off sparks and take fire, yield drops and flow, ring and tell of him".[44] The scholastic philosophers knew that we experience things intelligently by a *coordination* of our senses.

God's grandeur "gathers to a greatness, like the ooze of oil / Crushed". This comparison of the divine glory, at its most intense, to the oil issuing from crushed olives indicates that Hopkins's mind is moving along the track not only of creation but of redemption too. As the final lines of the poem make clear, the grandeur of God is expressed not least in his merciful loving-kindness. At the heart of the *Kyrie eleison*, the (Greek-language) call of the Roman liturgy for the mercy of God, is the beautiful word *eleos*, "mercy", which is close in sound to *elaia* ("olive") and

[43] *Letters,* 168–69.
[44] *Sermons,* 195.

elaion ("olive oil"). Possibly Hopkins was aware of the Renaissance paintings of the Mother and Child which include a vessel of oil as symbol of the future *Christus patiens,* the suffering Christ. From the crushed Fruit will flow the healing "unction"—for Scripture and Fathers a denomination of the Holy Spirit.[45] God's glory is nowhere more fully contemplated than in the saving sacrifice of his Son, since what is most magnificent about divine omnipotence is its unexpected love. Why, then, Hopkins asks, do not people take more notice of the glory of the Lord—of such a Lord—immanent in the created order? Why do they not "reck his rod"? Not reckon with his authority, but, given the closeness of "rod" to "rood"—another kind of stick—we can amplify this and say, they do not reckon with the authority of his love.

His answer is that "Generations have trod, have trod, have trod; / And all is seared with trade". The word "Generations" is unusually Latinate for Hopkins, whose preference for Anglo-Saxon roots was of a piece with his emphasis on the primordial—in this case, the primordially English tongue.[46] But precisely the formal dignity of "generations", which conjures up the panoply of history's march through time, underlines the contrast with the reality brought home in the repeated "have trod", where we sense the curse of

45 Certainly Hopkins was familiar with the cognate symbol of the Christ of the Passion as crushed grapes from a winepress: thus the early poem from his Anglican period, "Barnfloor and Winepress." In any case, these liturgical and iconographical monuments can be considered the objective correlate in sacred tradition of Hopkins's choice of words.

46 "His love of getting back to the origins of words was less an archaeological exercise than a real attempt to scrape clean the bones of language and restore its purity, which seems in retrospect to have a good deal to do with his attempt to go back in religion to the period when modern habits of thought had not contaminated it." Thus R. B. Martin, *Gerard Manley Hopkins,* 66.

tedious and unrelenting work in a fallen world. But if man suffers—ultimately, for a reader of Genesis, at his own hand, so does the earth: also at human hands. Man has disfigured the effects of God's creative act by his own flawed economic activity. Beyond the valley of the Clwyd, where Hopkins was writing, lay the Wales of the Industrial Revolution, with its mines and smelters. The South Walian valleys, indeed, would become a byword for the degradation of landscape. Economic advance is bought at a price. Mass production of goods may mean that men are "shod", but "being shod" could mean that "foot cannot feel"—not identify, with an appropriate degree of response, the feel of the earth and recognise it for what it is, the finite yet revealing medium of the glory of God.

The sonnet's sestet—its last six lines—has the *volta* or "turn" characteristic of this poetic form. It is not a *volte-face*, but it is, in comparison with what has gone before, a strikingly new thought. When Hopkins now tells us that, despite all this searing, "nature is never spent" owing to the "freshness" there is deep down, he is not referring to what the philosophers call *natura naturata*, the condition of the various species in their earthly habitat as the natural historian might assess it. He is referring, rather, to *natura naturans*, the "mother nature" of which at any given time, in any given place, the state of the natural world is the effect. And in so referring to what the ancient Greeks called *Phusis*—not, here, the nature of some particular thing but nature in its own font and source—he is doing so, as we soon go on to discover, not in a pagan fashion but in a specifically Christian one. True, the "last lights" may go out "off the black West". An industrialised earth may sink into night under a blanket of smog, just as in any case the daily fading of light leaves all colours pitch-dark. But the creative Trinity is at work as the ceaseless energy renewing *natura naturans* at its own matrix. Now for Christian orthodoxy, the Father is the unconditional source of that energy, the Son the container of its forms, the Holy Spirit its communicator in creation, the whole Trinity acting as one, yet differentiated by the roles the Three play thanks to their respective place in the Triune life. Here, then, it must be the Holy Spirit who is named. Hopkins does so name him in the way the opening verses of Genesis suggest and the Gospel accounts of the Baptism of Christ—that new moving of the "dove" over the waters—confirm. The scriptural symbolism of the Holy Spirit as *bird* enables Hopkins to invoke the Spirit's nurturing yet protecting love ("breast" and "wings"), and the warmth and radiance he ascribes to the third divine Person recover in his conclusion the qualities of the divine glory from which "God's Grandeur" set out. This is for the Holy Spirit a "bent" world, for two reasons. Not only is it a world warped out of true. It is also, whatever Victorian freethinkers might believe, a *creation* which has, then, an "obediential potency" to the divine transfiguring action: a world that, of its essence, bends before God's almighty doing. Hence the confidence with which this sonnet closes.

The Starlight Night

LOOK at the stars! look, look up at the stars!
  O look at all the fire-folk sitting in the air!
  The bright boroughs, the circle-citadels there!
Down in dim woods the diamond delves! the elves'-eyes!
The grey lawns cold where gold, where quickgold lies!
  Wind-beat whitebeam! airy abeles set on a flare!
  Flake-doves sent floating forth at a farmyard scare!—
Ah well! it is all a purchase, all is a prize.
Buy then! bid then!—What?—Prayer, patience, alms, vows.
Look, look: a May-mess, like on orchard boughs!
  Look! March-bloom, like on mealed-with-yellow sallows!
These are indeed the barn; withindoors house
The shocks. This piece-bright paling shuts the spouse
  Christ home, Christ and his mother and all his hallows.

·   ·   ·   ·   ·   ·   ·

This poem was written at St Beuno's on 24 February 1877. We know that Hopkins was susceptible to the clarity of a night sky where the stars are well defined. In his journals for 1874 he notes:

> As we drove home, the stars came out thick: I leant back to look at them and my heart opening more than usual praised the Lord to and in whom all that beauty comes home.[47]

---

[47] *Journals,* 254.

He was in southwest England when he wrote those words,
but the sky would hardly look less enchanting on a frosty
night in north Wales. Well-researched amateur astronomy,
such as Hopkins himself practised,[48] enables Norman
MacKenzie to write:

> In February from British latitudes one can see such sugges-
> tive patterns as sickle or u-shaped citadels in Leo and
> Corona Borealis, groups of stars like bright boroughs in the
> Pleaides and Orion, the long curved neck of Cygnus the
> Swan, which could be imagined a swirl of doves rising from
> the ground, Sirius so diamond-brilliant that it seems to
> change colour as it twinkles. Above all, the fascinating river
> of the Milky Way with its countless minute points of light
> lends itself to reveries.[49]

Hopkins's initial reverie is of a celestial campfire with the
"folk" inhabiting the stars making merry. The ancients considered the stars animated by divine movers, which in Christian Platonism become angelic movers. But this relatively
philosophical belief stands in sharp contrast to Hopkins's
fantasy of a populace in sober revelry. Perhaps, like J. R. R.
Tolkien in the following century, he was weaving strands of a
homemade mythology for the British who, insofar as they
ever had one, had lost it. Certainly one of the valuable functions of myth is to provide a language for a sense of the liv-
ingness of the cosmos in that organic unity where nothing is
without some correspondence to everything else. As the cita-
tion from MacKenzie suggests, the shapes of the various con-

---

48 Cf. ibid., 170: "Before sunrise looking out of a window saw a
noble scape of stars—the Plough all golden falling, Cassiopeia on
end with her bright quains pointing to the right, the graceful
bends of Perneus underneath her, and some great star whether
Capella or not I am not sure risen over the brow of the mountain."

49 N. H. MacKenzie, *A Reader's Guide to Gerard Manley Hopkins,* 67.

stellations fed Hopkins's imagination to the point that he
found himself looking down—as it were from a balloon (we
should say from a *spaceship*)—on an alternative world. To
Hopkins's delighted vision this "world" has its own town-
ships and walled cities. It has forests and grassland (here the
mistier nebulae are doubtless in mind) where drops of
golden dew shine. It has its quarries ("delves") where deposits
of gem-bearing ore are glinting. It even has another rational
species—elves—whose eyes are visible. (Truth of scale hardly
enters into such mythopoeic picturing.) And it has among
the constellations some that put him in mind of trees with
whitish leaves, at least on their underside: the sorbus or
whitebeam, and the abele or white poplar. Finally in the
octet, swirls of stars strike him as like flights of white doves,
themselves compared, as they settle again after lifting off in
fright from some commotion, to snowflakes: "Flake-doves
sent floating forth at a farmyard scare!"

The capacity to imagine alternative worlds and to popu-
late the real universe with their denizens is theologically
interesting. It testifies to the sub-creative potential of man,
which follows from his making in the divine image. "All
proportions guarded", as the French say, we can share in
the divine creativity not by originating things from nothing, which is an exclusively divine prerogative, but by
reassembling—in different media, of which fantasy is
one—the materials of the world. At the same time, the
actual imagining of a potential world brings home to us the
fact that the actual world we have—which once was itself
merely potential—is so marvellous. (G. K. Chesterton is
the great celebrator of this.) Hopkins himself registers the
ontological value of such imaginings when he writes, "Ah
well! it is all a purchase, all is a prize".

And that brings him to the sonnet's "turn". Through
"bidding", *praying* (the Prayers of the Faithful in the Roman

liturgy are known in England by the tautologous name of "bidding prayers"), to which Hopkins links a variety of moral and ascetic practices—"patience, alms, vows"—we can learn to see the radiant yet various beauty of the (actual, not fantasy) creation as symbolic of the heavenly beauty which lies beyond this world (and all possible alternative worlds). The massed stars, which Hopkins now compares to blossom in orchards in May time or the pussy willows so common in Britain in early spring, where they serve as a native equivalent to the palms of Passiontide, can be for us—if the right spiritual dispositions are ours—pointers to the lights of heaven. Hopkins understands "heaven", or the goal of human life, in an explicitly Christian fashion. Heaven is not only the vision of God taken *simpliciter*, though the mind's "seeing" God and "seeing" with him, through his own uncreated form, is the heart of it. More distinctively, the "life everlasting" of the Creed is the vision of God made known in his incarnate Son, and, with that Son, then, the joyful contemplation of those who are by grace his members and who, in the power of his Ascension, he takes home with him. That means first and foremost the Blessed Virgin Mary, but secondly it means all the saints. Using one of the great biblical images for the End, the wedding banquet of the Lamb, Hopkins portrays heaven as feasting in a well-lit hall, itself piled high with the "shocks" or sheaves that are the harvested good works of God's elect. The blaze of light within the heavenly world shows through in pricks of light in the visible world of here and now, like chinks in the woodwork of an inhabited homestead at evening. This "piece-bright paling" encloses the risen and ascended Bridegroom of the Church, "the spouse / Christ home". And that will be, then, since the Lord is never without those he took our humanity to save, "Christ and his mother and all his hallows".

Taking the octet and sestet of the sonnet together, this may be, as Father Christopher Devlin proposed, one of those comparatively few points in the poems where Hopkins's theological Scotism is relevant. For Scotus, God created the world as a setting for the redemptive work of Christ. "The worlds of angels and of men were created as fields for Christ, in which to exercise his adoration of the Father, fields for him to sow and work and harvest".[50] By "establishing the purpose of God's creative act as genesis in Christ", Scotus had "hoped . . . to show the unity and perfection of the divine concern for creatures".[51] That was Hopkins's hope too.

---

[50] *Sermons,* 109.
[51] J. F. Cotter, *Inscape. The Christology and Poetry of Gerard Manley Hopkins* (Pittsburgh 1972), 122.

Spring

NOTHING is so beautiful as Spring—
    When weeds, in wheels, shoot long and lovely and lush;
    Thrush's eggs look little low heavens, and thrush
Through the echoing timber does so rinse and wring
The ear, it strikes like lightnings to hear him sing;
    The glassy peartree leaves and blooms, they brush
    The descending blue; that blue is all in a rush
With richness; the racing lambs too have fair their fling.

What is all this juice and all this joy?
    A strain of the earth's sweet being in the beginning
In Eden garden—Have, get, before it cloy,

    Before it cloud, Christ, lord, and sour with sinning,
Innocent mind and Mayday in girl and boy,
    Most, O maid's child, thy choice and worthy the winning.

· · · · · · ·

This poem was written at St Beuno's in the May of 1877. A sonnet in praise of Spring, it finds that season, and the yearly renewal of nature it brings in the northern hemisphere, a continuing effect of the Paradise garden of earth before the Fall of the human species. Though poems about springtime are ten a penny, this thought cannot be called commonplace—and in any case the glory of its working out is in the detail.

    At the hands of writers deprived of a metaphysical context for their work, the opening line could be platitudinous.

Of course "nothing"—no season—"is as beautiful as Spring".
Hopkins, working with a transcendental concept of beauty
(after all, he remarked of a bluebell that he knew "the beauty
of our Lord by it"),[52] is conscious of the web of being that
joins natural beauty to divine, finite to infinite beauty. This is
something arguably better expressed by Thomism, with its
"analogical" concept of the transcendentals, than it is by Scotism. But Hopkins's sense of being is informed by his
(broadly) Thomistic Jesuit training as well as by certain specific insights or claims of the Scotist school. And so it is that,
at his hands, the word "beauty" tingles with theological
expectation. How can we understand the further, Godward,
meaning of such a superlative beauty on earth? As yet, the
octet of the sonnet does not tell us, since Hopkins wants first
to bring home to us with all the force of observed and
reflected "inscape" what that vernal beauty entails.

It is characteristic of Hopkins's wonderful quirkiness that,
seeking a striking epiphany of spring in the realm of plant
life, he settles on none of the "flowers that bloom in the
spring"[53] but on spring's *weeds*. But do weeds wheel, precisely? Perhaps if their heads consist in whorls, they might.
But the very next word is a verb suggestive of dynamic action
and not simply static presentation: "*shoot* long and lovely and
lush". W. H. Gardner, editor of the third (1948) edition of
his poems and co-editor of the fourth (1963), points out that
notable among the weeds that really do "shoot" in "wheels"
are the "regular arcs" of the blackberry stems so common in
English hedgerows.[54] His fellow editor from the fourth edi-

---

[52] *Journals*, 199.

[53] The phrase stands for an overworked symbol of loveliness in W. S.
Gilbert's comic libretto for *The Mikado*. Hopkins, incidentally,
was a fan of Gilbert and Sullivan.

[54] W. H. Gardner, *Gerard Manley Hopkins: A Study of Poetic Idio-
syncrasy in Relation to Poetic Tradition* (London 1962, 2nd edition), II, 238.

tion, Norman MacKenzie, makes an alternative—and typically brilliant—suggestion: brilliant because it carries us over to the other exempla of spring life the poem contains. In fountains, water certainly "wheels". So, seen from above, the "radiating leaves and stems" of weeds of all kinds might seem like just such a cascade.[55] The motif of *fluidity*—for spring is when sap rises and nature's juices flow again—may then be said to continue in the poet's further observations. Hopkins speaks of how "thrushes' eggs look [like] little low heavens", as it were pools of bluey water reflecting the colour of the sky. And of how too the call of the thrush through the woodland "does . . . rinse" the ear like a jet of water cleansing it from the wax that impedes our hearing.

That cry of the bird comes ringing—but Hopkins once again deliberately disrupts our conventional habits of attention to nature by using for a verb not "ring" but "wring". The sound of these two words is, of course, identical, and so the poet can strike two notes at once. There are not only the bell-like tones of the birdsong. There is also the way it invades us and compels to notice its "lightnings". And so, looking upward and outward—by implication, our perceptual horizon is now broadened, we see the "descending blue" of the sky, brushed by the pearly blossoms of the peartrees, and across the fields lambs not merely gambolling, a word, which, just because it denotes strictly lamb-ish behaviour, would add little, but, rather, having a "fling"—as though they were taking part in a traditional folk dance such as the "Highland Fling" of the Scots. (Country dancing in England—and Wales—would have been much more common in Hopkins's day than ours.)

The poet's question is, then, in the sestet: "What is all this juice?" And his answer is, it is "a strain of the earth's sweet

---

55 N. H. MacKenzie, *A Reader's Guide to Gerard Manley Hopkins*, 69.

being in the beginning / In Eden garden". We must note the
ambiguity of "strain". Music, when it avoids cacophony, has
sweet strains—and Hopkins, whose favourite composer was
Purcell, could probably not have imagined the sonic revolution worked by Schoenberg and Berg. So this flurry of gor-
geous, flowing movement after the frozen sluggishness of
winter is an echo, or a reprise, of the "music"—the delightful vitality—of the prelapsarian world. But the word
"strain" also suggests the key Hopkinsian term "stress". We
are dealing here not merely with the symbolic afterlife of
Paradise but with the continuing consequences of the
divine creative energy invested there. The Paradisal "instress"
of God's sustaining and ultimately engracing activity is still
at work in the world. Hopkins has alerted us in advance to
the theme of that engracing when he spoke of the "rush" of
the blue heavens descending through the blossoming
boughs of the trees: a pointer to the downward flow of
grace from God to men.

But now with the sonnet's *volta* Hopkins discloses the
Christological context which alone gives spring awakening its
full force in human life. Using tones of great urgency, he calls
on Christ to guard the Paradisal "strain" in the minds and
hearts of children—humanity's newly sprung ones—before
innocent minds have a chance to cloud over with sin and
hearts be soured by it. In classical Catholic theology it is usual
to find the results of original sin in an obfuscation of the
intellect and a corruption of the will—its turning, as soured
milk is said to turn. Christ must "have" and "get" while there
is still time "innocent mind and Mayday in girl and boy".

Hopkins may be thinking of preservation in innocence
through the "actual" or moment-by-moment graces which
God's providence furnishes. Or, more radically, he might be
envisaging here the gift of sanctifying—habitual—grace in
Baptism, whereby a little one becomes a child of God and

inheritor of the kingdom of heaven. The doctrine of Baptism speaks of the active restoring of the primeval innocence in the regenerated child, as he or she dons the robe of grace, symbolised by the white garment put on the newly baptised after their dipping in the waters of the font. There the reign of concupiscence is broken, and any persistence of its remnants, which now become stimuli to holy warfare, is a token of the soul's supernatural renewal in innocence. Or, finally, Hopkins may have in mind that "prevenient grace" whose property it is to prepare the will to receive whatever graces of conversion may follow. In his commentary on the Ignatian *Exercises*, he compares *gratia praeveniens* with the grace received by spiritual creatures in the first moment of the aboriginal creation. That is manifestly pertinent to "Spring".

> God's forestalling of man's action by prevenient grace, which carries with it a consenting of man's will, seems to stand to the action of free choice which follows and to which, by its continued strain and breathing on man's responding aspiration or drawing in of breath, it leads / as the creation of men and angels in sanctifying grace stands to the act by which they entered with God into the covenant and commonwealth of original justice; further / as the infused virtues of baptism stand to the acts of faith etc which long after follow.[56]

The comparison with the creation in Eden gives this third possibility a special congruence. In "imitation of Spring's straining action", Hopkins is asking for the "strain of the will" to be grafted onto the "strain of God's grace ordained from creation".[57] In the personal vocabulary Hopkins worked out

56 *Sermons*, 157.
57 M. Raiger, "'Poised but on the Quiver': The Paradox of Free Will and Grace in Hopkins's 'Spring' and 'Carrion Comfort'", *Religion and the Arts* 3:1 (1999): 64–95, and here at 72.

in his notebooks for the doctrine of grace, this would be not so much "correcting" grace or "elevating" grace (itself a classical theological term). Rather would it be "quickening" grace, seen by him as "stimulating, towards the object, towards good".[58] In any case, in one way or another, Hopkins is praying that there be in these children some preservation of what was otherwise lost with the Fall. For Hopkins's Scotus-influenced doctrine of the Incarnation this will be a presence of the Christ, who was "preordained to become human even without the commission of sin".[59]

He may have chosen to become a human infant on Mary's lap whether or not there was a Fall. Grace now, however, in all its aspects is the outflow of the Victory of Christ over sin and death. There was a choice according to the eternal counsels of God. There was also a winning. And if we ask what was in view in each, one clue is his own declaration that the divine kingdom belongs above all to "little children" (Matthew 18:3; 19:14). An entire theology of spiritual childhood lies subjacent here. Hence the sonnet's final line: "Most, O maid's child, thy choice and worthy the winning".

---

58 *Sermons*, 158.
59 M. Raiger, " 'Poised but on the Quiver' ", 73.

The Windhover: To Christ our Lord

I CAUGHT this morning, morning's minion, king-
    dom of daylight's dauphin, dapple-dawn-drawn Falcon, in
        his riding
    Of the rolling level underneath him steady air, and striding
High there, how he rung upon the rein of a wimpling wing
In his ecstasy! then off, off forth on swing,
    As a skate's head sweeps smooth on a bow-bend: the hurl and
        gliding
    Rebuffed the big wind. My heart in hiding
Stirred for a bird,—the achieve of, the mastery of the thing!

Brute beauty and valour and act, oh, air, pride, plume, here
    Buckle! AND the fire that breaks from thee then, a billion
Times told lovelier, more dangerous, O my chevalier!

    No wonder of it: shéer plód makes plough down sillion
Shine, and blue-break embers, ah my dear,
    Fall, gall themselves, and gash gold-vermilion.

.   .   .   .   .   .

Written at St Beuno's on 30 May 1877, many commentators, including Hopkins himself, at any rate at mid career,
have seen this as his finest poem. It is certainly among the
most written about. Hopkins opens by describing how,
leaving, or at least looking out from, St Beuno's one morning, he "caught"—caught sight of—the flight of a kestrel
or "windhover", a dialect term for this bird of prey of the

falcon family, which does indeed seem to hover in the air prior to swooping down or off again. On the basis of ornithological sources, MacKenzie explains that these birds require "almost computer-speed responses" to wind variations since "to remain stationary over one spot they have to fly into the wind at exactly its own speed", their wings quivering—or, as Hopkins writes, "wimpling"—in a controlled yet rapid fashion, "missing a few beats as gusts die, accelerating as they freshen".[60] Evidently the name "windhover" is a well-chosen one.

Hopkins was suitably impressed by this mastery which the octet of the poem with a seeming effortlessness reproduces in the medium of words. Hopkins notes the bird's "riding / Of the rolling level underneath him steady air", his "striding high there". He marvels at how the kestrel "rung upon the rein of a wimpling wing / In his ecstasy!" and then was off again: "off forth on swing", and how "the hurl and gliding / Rebuffed the big wind". Such is the identification with the dynamic pattern of the bird's movement that we can surely say, this is no *mere* catching sight of. Rather, Hopkins grasped the "inscape" of the kestrel's characteristic flight. Hence his heart "stirred"—and not only at this wonder of the world of birds. Even if we lacked the poem's dedication ("To Christ our Lord"), the opening description of the windhover would tell us that the subject of the poem is not simply a diurnal species of bird-life. True, Hopkins stresses how the bird belongs with the daylight hours. The windhover is "*morning's* minion", "*kingdom of daylight's* dauphin", "*dapple-dawn-drawn* Falcon". But the substantives which the adjectival forms qualify are in the first two cases, *minion* and *dauphin*, human—the kestrel is a "favourite", as at a king's court—a "minion", and

---

60 N. H. MacKenzie, *A Reader's Guide to Gerard Manley Hopkins,* 77.

is itself a royal figure like the dauphin, the heir to the French crown. And in the third case— *"Falcon"*—the capitalised noun tells us that more than avian admiration is in question. Hopkins sees the falcon as a knight riding on horseback, drawn to the sun-king (a well-known title of the greatest of French monarchs, Louis XIV), just as "dawn"— "dapple-dawn-drawn"—leads inexorably to the sunshine of full day.

In the sestet the implications of the octet and opening dedication combined are set out for us. From the spectacle of the bird's magnificent perfection, as Hopkins, entranced, watches that perfection in act: "Brute beauty and valour and act, oh, air, pride, plume, here / Buckle!", there breaks forth, he tells us, a "fire". That is language we have learned to associate, in Hopkins's writing, with divine epiphany. What irrupts here is a stupendous revelation of the "chevalier" to whom the sonnet is devoted, Christ himself, whose intrinsic splendour and energetic action are of a different order of magnitude altogether: " a billion / Times told lovelier, more dangerous". As Donald McChesney writes, Hopkins addresses the words "O my chevalier!" *through* the falcon to Christ.[61] All the superb qualities of the windhover, we heard, "buckle": that is, they fuse into a flash of recognition that, through this very inscape, the order of nature points to the supernatural order, which, in the divine intention, precedes it, and, in the order of value, exceeds it far. As the Canticle of Zechariah records, Jesus Christ is the "Dayspring that visits us from on high" (Luke 1:78), the true "morning's minion".

In the last tercet of the poem, Hopkins adduces reasons why one ought not to be surprised that the Lord can make use of wild nature for his self-revelation—and wild nature,

[61] D. McChesney, *A Hopkins Commentary*, 68.

accordingly, surrender its own significance to make way for his. There is a seam of sacrifice running through all things. Just so hard agrarian toil makes the fields shine with golden crops for the harvest ("shéer plód makes plough down sillion / Shine"), and the human heart, often reduced to apparent ashes, to "blue-bleak embers", run with its own facsimile of the saving blood that flowed from the side of Christ. Just as from his side, gashed by the soldier's spear (John 19:34), there flowed forth the blood and water which the Fathers saw as the streams of baptismal and Eucharistic grace that found the Church and save the world, so from man, a natural creature but now through Christ wonderfully engraced, sacrificial living can produce a share in his salvation, a reclothing of the self in the heraldic colours, the splendid "gold-vermilion", of the King. It is a controlling conviction of the Gospel of St John, whose Passion narrative includes the episode of the piercing, that the "kenosis" or self-emptying of the Saviour did not conceal but further revealed his glory. As Hopkins himself put it in his sermons:

> Poor was his station, laborious his life, bitter his ending: through poverty, through labour, through crucifixion his majesty of nature more shines.[62]

---

[62] *Sermons*, 37.

Pied Beauty

GLORY be to God for dappled things—
 For skies of couple-colour as a brinded cow;
  For rose-moles all in stipple upon trout that swim;
Fresh-firecoal chestnut-falls; finches' wings;
 Landscape plotted and pierced—fold, fallow, and plough;
  And áll trádes, their gear and tackle and trim.
All things counter, original, spare, strange;
 Whatever is fickle, freckled (who knows how?)
  With swift, slow; sweet, sour; adazzle, dim;
He fathers-forth whose beauty is past change:
                    Praise him.

· · · · · · ·

Written at St Beuno's in the summer of 1877, this sonnet, one of Hopkins's best known, could well be taken to illustrate the Jesuit motto 'To the Greater Glory of God', or—even better—its Benedictine equivalent (at the Oratory school, Hopkins had considered becoming a Benedictine), "In All Things may God be Glorified". All is compressed, because this is a sonnet only by way of its proportions: Hopkins invented for it the name of a "curtal" sonnet, on the analogy of a small breed of horse which has this name. The meaning of the title, "Pied Beauty", needs no comment, since the poem is its explication.

  Hopkins's love of unexpected diversity in nature and nurture (human culture) expands into speech in the opening exclamation, "Glory be to God for dappled things"—that is, for the rich patchwork of nature's colouring. His first example of this chromatic beauty is the sky, of which he was a close observer, not only through his interest in astronomy but, even more, as a Ruskinian. For the young John Ruskin had made his reputation (one cannot say "his name" since his early work was anonymous) through his gift of transposing into verbal description the skyscapes—even more than the seascapes and landscapes—of Turner. Hopkins's journals emulate Ruskin in their concentrated attention to Britain's variegated skies. And this sets the tone, which is, precisely, "couple-colour": in the streaked or two-coloured ("brinded") cattle to which Hopkins compares certain British skyscapes; in the pink stippling on the skin of (grey-brown) trout, one of the most sought-after freshwater fish of the North Atlantic islands; in the glowing red of (brown-black) chestnuts as they come off the brazier (hot-chestnut sellers were a frequent sight in Victorian towns and cities in the colder months), and, more predictably, in the plumage of different sorts of finches, of which Hopkins's country could boast a wide variety. (There is something litany-like about these lists in Hopkins's poetry, which Father Ian Ker has compared to the litanic prayers which were a feature of Victorian Catholic devotion, in sharp contrast to the elaborately composed continuous prose of the orations in the Anglican *Book of Common Prayer*.)[63]

That is nature. But nature has its proper continuation in culture, since it is *man's* nature to work over the given of non-human nature, cultivating it in senses both literal and metaphorical. So without a pause, Hopkins moves directly into corresponding "pied beauty" in the world of distinctively human making. The combined effect of pasture land,

---

63 I. Ker, *The Catholic Revival in English Literature 1845–1961: Newman, Hopkins, Belloc, Chesterton, Greene, Waugh* (Leominster 2003).

fields that are fallow, and fields currently under cultivation—"fold, fallow and plough"—is to give even (or especially) a flat agrarian countryside a delightfully "pied"
appearance. It is "plotted and pieced". And as for the earth
on which the countryman works so also for the tools with
which he works. Hopkins was always interested in the tool-
kits of different trades and the specialised vocabulary, some
of it very ancient, craftsmen used for their contents. The
"gear and tackle" of all trades reflects and perpetuates created diversity.[64]

Then, in what would correspond in a classic sonnet to
the sestet, but here the lines are only four, Hopkins both
generalises and theologises. Colour is not the only pleasing
contrast. Before the poem ends, Hopkins will mention at
least three more: speed, tastingness, and luminosity. Contrasts of many sorts, some of them less superficial than the
chromatic (though can the epiphany of created forms in
their self-presentation ever rightly be called "superficial"?),
run through the world of nature, making it frequently
"counter, original, spare, strange".

So much for the generalisation. But what of the theology?
It forms the conclusion which, by its doxological character,
also returns us to the poem's beginning. "He fathers-forth
whose beauty is past change: / Praise him". The poet finds
the source of the world's contrasting beauties to lie in the
generativity of the divine Father whose own beauty is
changeless, unlike the cascade of things that come into being
and pass away again. Hopkins may have been thinking of
Augustine's naming God in the *Confessions* as the Beauty that
is ever-old yet ever-new, just because he is *eternal* Beauty,

---

[64] Hopkins would have known from his study of Thomism that for
Aquinas the ultimate unity can be imitated only by the multiplic-
ity of things: a point made in J. G. Lawler, *Hopkins Re-constructed*,
149.

transcending all the mutability in this-worldly beauty while also enabling it by non-competitively letting it be. We might venture a comment on "fathers-forth" based this time not on the Latin patristic tradition but on the Greek. It is because God is eternally Father—eternally Source of the only-begotten Son—that we know him to be of his nature utter generous productivity. His world is not a fluke, or an arbitrary decision of the divine will, but the real reflection of the Father's everlasting being.

Hurrahing in Harvest

SUMMER ends now; now, barbarous in beauty, the stooks rise
Around; up above, what wind-walks! what lovely
        behaviour
Of silk-sack clouds! has wilder, wilful-wavier
Meal-drift moulded ever and melted across skies?

I walk, I lift up, I lift up heart, eyes,
Down all that glory in the heavens to glean our Saviour;
And, éyes, heárt, what looks, what lips yet gave you a
Rapturous love's greeting of realer, of rounder replies?

And the azurous hung hills are his world-wielding shoulder
Majestic—as a stallion stalwart, very-violet-sweet!—
These things, these things were here and but the beholder
Wanting; which two when they once meet,
The heart rears wings bold and bolder
And hùrls for him, O half hurls earth for him off under his
        feet.

·   ·   ·   ·   ·   ·   ·

This is another St Beuno's poem, dating this time from the
opening day of September in 1877. To approach its startling
imagery—and theme—aright we could do worse than take
as a guide a soberly concise theological assertion Hopkins
would make five years later in the "Further Notes on the
Foundation" contained in his *Sermons and Devotional Writings*. There Hopkins wrote:

God's utterance of himself in himself is God the Word, outside himself is this world. This world then is word, expression, news of God.[65]

What we shall find in "Hurrahing the Harvest" is an overwhelming poetic application of that lapidary truth.

When the poem opens, on the cusp between summertime and fall, Hopkins is filled with exultation at the evidence of nature's vigour and loveliness. Describing the circumstances of the poem's genesis to his friend Bridges, he called it the outcome of an "extreme enthusiasm" as he walked back to the Jesuit college from a day's fishing in the valley of the Elwy.[66] In the octet two things strike him: the harvested wheat fields and the condition of the sky. He registers the wheat-sheaves ("stooks"), propped up in standing groups which put him in mind—at least this is Norman MacKenzie's proposal—of "grass-skirted tribesmen".[67] Hence "barbarous in beauty, the stooks rise / Around". Looking up, he sees the clouds scudding down the "wind-walks", as though along celestial avenues formed by the currents of air that carry them along. Drawing on his long-honed habits of exact observing, he notes two distinct types of cloud, one rather glossier than the cumulus clouds sometimes called woolpacks—hence "silk-sack clouds"—and another, presumably cirrocumulus, high above them, shape-shifting into "wilful-wavier / Meal-drift".

Now comes the first shock to the sensibility. Hopkins starts to "glean", as though, after the manner of peasants, scavenging for edible remains in the harvested corn. But his gleaning takes place not in the fields but "down all that

---

65 *Sermons*, 129.
66 Cited N. H. MacKenzie, *A Reader's Guide to Gerard Manley Hopkins*, 88.
67 Ibid.

glory in the heavens". And what he gleans is Jesus Christ. With an extraordinary mystical realism, he pronounces the "greeting" he receives through the cloudscape from the Saviour to be a "realer" and "rounder" reply than his eyes and heart have ever received from other—simply human— "looks" and "lips". Appealing to a favoured technical term in the patristic and medieval and Counter-Reformation vocabulary of Catholic mysticism, his explanation is that the greeting in question expresses "Rapturous love". Here the cosmos above—the heavens—becomes the medium for the Word's kiss of the soul.

The sestet moves us further on. Gazing now at the hills that enclose the valley, Hopkins takes in both their impressive dimensions and the delicate tones that are theirs from the declining sun. Not only does he combine these contrasting qualities, imaged as those of a powerful horse on the one hand, the fragile violet on the other. He also sees in this combination the might and the gentleness of the saving Word—who is none other than the creating Word whose being these hills reveal. "And the azurous hung hills are his world-wielding shoulder / Majestic, as a stallion stalwart, very-violet-sweet!". This is no mere symbolism, it is *symbolic realism*, for, as Hopkins goes on to add: "these things were here and but the beholder / Wanting". What more simply stated rejection of Idealism, or indeed of a non-symbolic realism, could there be? But now they have their beholder, the poet himself. And so they can attain their proper effect, which is—precisely—*raptus*, a rapture in which as the heart "rears wings" he feels himself rising like Pegasus, the winged horse of antiquity, to meet his Lord in the sky. Curiously, St Paul in the First Letter to the Thessalonians had imagined the final Parousia of Christ as some such midair encounter (4:17). Hopkins is aware that no fundamental alteration in the relation of our space-time to that of the God-man in his risen and ascended state is at issue here. That is why he writes that the heart "*half* hurls earth for him off under his feet". Still, the disclosure of the Word in the heavens is now completed by a comparable rapture-inducing disclosure, on the earth.

Justus George Lawler holds that the whole poem constitutes a Romantic gloss on Psalm 19, which opens with the cry: "The heavens are telling the glory of God" (verse 1a); and goes on to speak of how divine words have gone out "through all the earth" (verse 4a), "to the end of the world" (verse 4b), before describing the course followed by the sun across these vast spaces. The Christian exegesis of the Psalter understands this by reference to:

> the Sun of Justice, the Saviour, who 'comes forth like the groom' from the bridal chamber, and is like an Atlantean giant ('world-wielding shoulder') 'joyfully running his course' [verse 5].[68]

The kiss of the Logos is given first from the heavens but then from the earth itself, and that is possible because he is "the cosmically unifying incarnational Word".[69]

---

[68] J. G. Lawler, *Hopkins Re-constructed*, 241.
[69] Ibid., 243.

The Lantern out of Doors

SOMETIMES a lantern moves along the night.
  That interests our eyes. And who goes there?
  I think; where from and bound, I wonder, where,
With, all down darkness wide, his wading light?

Men go by me whom either beauty bright
  In mould or mind or what not else makes rare:
  They rain against our much-thick and marsh air
Rich beams, till death or distance buys them quite.

Death or distance soon consumes them: wind
  What most I may eye after, be in at the end
I cannot, and out of sight is out of mind.

Christ minds: Christ's interest, what to avow or amend
  There, éyes them, heart wánts, care haúnts, foot fóllows kínd,
Their ránsom, théir rescue, ánd first, fást, last friénd.

·   ·   ·   ·   ·   ·   ·

A St Beuno's poem from March or April 1877, "The Lantern
out of Doors", like its Oxonian companion piece, "The Candle Indoors", of two years later, will reassure those who are
worried lest Hopkins's finding God and his Word Jesus
Christ in nature is to the exclusion of any concentration of
interest on other human beings—who are, assuredly, part of
nature but also transcend nature. It is one of a number of
Hopkins's poems that can reasonably be called *priestly*.

At a time when city streets were laboriously gas-lit, the Victorian countryside was deeply dark at night, not least in far away corners of Wales. Hopkins reminds his readers it is not so unusual a thing to see a lantern winding its way through the pitch. He finds himself speculating about the identity, the whence, and the whither of the person carrying this "wading light"—here the adjective summons up a sense of the many resistances human beings must force their way through if they are to make progress on their pilgrimage.

People can be themselves radiant beams of light in the social murk. With his feeling for the multivalency of beauty, for which neither the term "physical" nor the term "spiritual" by itself will do, Hopkins knows there are those whom "either beauty bright / In mould or mind or what not else makes rare". The word "mould" is, probably deliberately, ambiguous, since it can signify either body-shape or the soul, which, for the scholastic philosophers, following Aristotle, is the form of the body. Hopkins is pointing toward a quality of radiance that has its supreme expression in the graces of transfiguration given, even on earth, to certain saints. Touches of it, however, can be discerned in many lives. That rare beauty—"rare", then, not so much because it is unusual but because it is precious—is as real, in itself and in its effects, as is the weather. Such men "rain" a light of their own—"rich beams"—that alter the makeup of the human atmosphere, "our much-thick and marsh air". (Probably Hopkins prefaced "thick" by "much" rather than the more grammatically correct "very" so as to convey a sense of clottedness.) But alas, "death or distance buys them quite". Biological death or the severance of companionship through removal to far-off places put an end to this benign effect on oneself quite as successfully as would their sale into slavery. Indeed, they are for all practical purposes "consumed"—reduced to nothing, like the ashes of the departed on a Hindu burial pyre.

Hopkins ends the first half of the sonnet's sestet by lamenting that, try as he will to follow their succeeding course, the eye of the watchfully concerned mind loses them utterly. The movement of the poet's thought, which, though hardly complex, is subtly expressed in unusual syntax, comes down with a bump in a commonplace proverb that sums the situation up: "out of sight is out of mind". But just here—rather than at the conventional point in the classic sonnet form—comes the true "turn" of his thinking on this topic. There is one to whom these limitations of perception and of love do not apply. "Christ minds": and the word "minds" is charged here, meaning at once that he remembers, he is concerned, and he conceives or understands. A passage of an 1880 sermon reads:

> God knows infinite things, all things, and heeds them all in particular. We cannot 'do two things at once', that is cannot give our full heed and attention to two things at once. God heeds all things at once. He takes more interest in a merchant's business than the merchant, in a vessel's steering than the pilot, in a lover's sweetheart than the lover, in a sick man's pain than the sufferer, in our salvation than we ourselves.[70]

It is a passage that lacks the explicitly Christological focus of the closing trio of lines of "The Lantern out of Doors", but for the orthodox Hopkins, Christ is always God as well as man. The 1882 sermon reproduces that *interested* character of divine omniscience which the poem stresses. Hopkins the preacher ascribes to God a passionately interested all-knowingness, and Hopkins the poet emphasises the far from disinterested character of Christ's minding those who

---

70 *Sermons*, 89.

go beyond our picture frame. "Christ's interest, what to avow or amend / There, éyes them". This is God as what the medievals called *humanissimus Salvator*, our "very human Saviour" who, consonant with his perfect grasp of the natural and supernatural human good, knows both what to confirm in our lives and what should be changed there. Hopkins intensifies the sense of this proactive, engaged divine-human attention with the verbs that follow: "heart wánts, care haúnts, foot fóllows kínd". And this is what we should expect if Christ really is the Saviour of man: "Their ránsom, théir rescue". And Hopkins adds, in a final soteriological reference that brings together the Victorian cult of friendship with the traditional theology of the saving Incarnation as the inclusion of man within the divine friendship (thus Aelred of Rievaulx, thus Thomas Aquinas): 'ánd first, fást, last friénd'.

The May Magnificat

MAY is Mary's month, and I
Muse at that and wonder why:
    Her feasts follow reason,
    Dated due to season—

Candlemas, Lady Day;
But the Lady Month, May,
    Why fasten that upon her,
    With a feasting in her honour?

Is it only its being brighter
Than the most are must delight her?
    Is it opportunest
    And flowers finds soonest?

Ask of her, the mighty mother:
Her reply puts this other
    Question: What is Spring?—
    Growth in everything—

Flesh and fleece, fur and feather,
Grass and greenworld all together;
    Star-eyed strawberry-breasted
    Throstle above her nested.

Cluster of bugle blue eggs thin
Forms and warms the life within;
    And bird and blossom swell
    In sod or sheath or shell.

All things rising, all things sizing
Mary sees, sympathising
    With that world of good,
    Nature's motherhood.

Their magnifying of each its kind
With delight calls to mind
    How she did in her stored
    Magnify the Lord.

Well but there was more than this:
Spring's universal bliss
    Much, had much to say
    To offering Mary May.

When drop-of-blood-and-foam-dapple
Bloom lights the orchard-apple
    And thicket and thorp are merry
    With silver-surfèd cherry

And azuring-over greybell makes
Wood banks and brakes wash set like lakes
    And magic cuckoocall
    Caps, clears, and clinches all—

This ecstasy all through mothering earth
Tells Mary her mirth till Christ's birth
    To remember and exultation
    In God who was her salvation.

    .   .   .   .

This poem was written at Stonyhurst in May 1878. Hopkins himself did not care for it greatly, perhaps because it comes closest of his mature poems to mainstream Victorian poetic diction and "decorum"—though not so close that it proved acceptable to the taste of his religious superiors. By custom of the house, such poems—though hardly of the quality of Hopkins's tribute—were offered by the Stony-hurst Jesuits to the Mother of God during the month of May, which in nineteenth-century Catholic practice (and later) was set aside for special devotion in her honour. The difficulty of saying just why that particular month should be selected for that purpose—for any reason more weighty, one supposes, than a play on the similarity of the words "Mary" and "May"—is the poet's departure point. Normally, writes Hopkins, the major Marian feasts in their timing "follow reason, / Dated due to season", and he mentions by way of example the two closest in date to May: the Purification of the Virgin Mary on 2nd February, forty days after the birth of Jesus, a date fixed by the ritual provisions for new mothers of the Mosaic Torah, and the Annunciation of the Virgin on 25th March, exactly nine months before that birth at Christmas. (Incidentally, Hopkins could not have said so with such assurance had he been writing a century later, since the Roman Calendar of 1969 restructured these festivals as feasts of the Lord—Christ himself—rather than his Mother.) But what, then, can be the rationale for singling out May as a Marian month?

Is it, asks Hopkins, because sunlight is strongest then? Or is that month in some general sense most opportune—meaning, presumably, in a pedestrian sense of the word, convenient, the devotions of other months having been otherwise, and with better reason, assigned? Or again, is it simply that flowers are most readily available then? Like the secular equivalent, the crowning of a local girl as "the May-queen", Marian processions and the coronation of Marian statues were—and where they survive still are—simultaneously flower festivals, where floral garlands and other tributes played and play a major part. Hopkins opines that, were we

to ask the Mother of Jesus herself, she would give a rather
different answer, throwing back to ourselves a question: the
question, namely, "What is Spring?"

Much of the poem is taken up with showing the perti-
nence of this rhetorical question. Spring means "Growth in
everything", just as in Mary's divine motherhood—the first
dogma concerning her to be proclaimed, at the Council of
Ephesus of 431, and the foundation of all her other duties
and privileges—the infant Messiah was, in that first springtime of his human existence, himself growing in her womb.
Beasts and birds, and plant life of every description are
springing into new life in Maytime. Inevitably, when thinking of the spring landscape, Hopkins has to mention the
colour "green", and he does so in a—readily intelligible—
coining of his own, "greenworld". But the Marian colour
par excellence is blue. And maybe this is why he homes in
more especially on the thrush, or "throstle", seen "above her
nested / Cluster of bugle blue eggs thin". "*Bugle* blue"
because of the plant of that name, a native of woodland
and damp grassland, so Peter Mabey's *Flora Britannica*
informs us, whose "blue flowers . . . stand out against dark
leaves whose colour is hard to pin down".[71]

As Hopkins envisages her, the new exalted Mary—
assumed into heaven—looks with sympathy on this
panorama of "all things sizing", new life burgeoning, burst-
ing forth. He has confidence that he can ascribe this
response to the Mother of the Lord because nature's motherhood—itself analogous to the motherhood of grace which
is hers—is in and of itself a "world of good". In the Old Testament the first Genesis account of creation portrays the
Creator as pronouncing all his works "very good", and the
Thomist metaphysics Hopkins studied in his Jesuit training

[71] P. Mabey, *Flora Britannica* (London 1986), 316.

takes as a key concept the "convertibility" of being and goodness. All being, insofar as it is being, is good. To this claim of Christian scholasticism must be added the further axiom that the world of nature and the world of grace cannot be at loggerheads, since grace builds on nature and perfects it. Admittedly, this process is not without its tensions for those who are still in via, on their temporal pilgrimage of self-making. But that consideration hardly applies to the Madonna, who, assumed into heaven in integrity of body as well as soul, views the creation from the standpoint of one in whom its two orders are wholly and triumphantly united.

At this juncture Hopkins turns to develop thoughts stimulated by the title he has given this poem—thoughts which, in the poetic medium, also justify that title. Each natural form by its very existence "magnifies the Lord", to cite the words of Mary herself from the Lucan Magnificat (Luke 1:46). *The Benedicite*, or Song of the Three Young Men, drawn from the Book of Daniel in its longer Alexandrian recension (Daniel 3:56–88) and one of the most frequently used scriptural canticles of the Roman Office, turns largely on this outpouring of mute praise from the subrational creation—from the plants of the earth to the sea-creatures, the birds of heaven, and "beasts, both wild and tame". This cosmic glorification of God on the part of the cosmos takes place simply by virtue of things existing and acting according to their kinds. Hopkins's willingness to apply the language of "selvedness" to the non-personal world probably intensified his sense of this chorus in its marvellous diversity: "their magnifying of each its kind"—which might be considered a Scotist flourish added to a Thomist ontology. This orchestration of praise puts the Mother of the Lord in mind of her own "magnifying" of God and increases her joy.

This is not, however, all. Spring entails for nature "universal bliss". Airbrushed out of the picture, so one might object, is Tennysonian nature "red in tooth and claw". But for a metaphysics of creation, the good of the universe surpasses the good of any one of its parts, or of those parts taken severally. To that extent Hopkins is justified in selecting those features of "mothering earth", which best represent this cosmic flourishing: apple and fruit blossom, and the sea of bluebells that turns a grey landscape azure, making "Wood banks and brakes wash wet like lakes". For him, the "magic cuckoocall" here "Caps, clears, and clinches all", constituting the *quod erat demonstrandum* of this particular argument in theodicy. But Hopkins has not yet explained the Marian significance of this "ecstasy". It is that it "Tells Mary her mirth till Christ's birth", and the "exultation" in God her Saviour, which, for the original Magnificat of St Luke's Gospel, is a parallelism of a typically Hebraic kind to her "magnification" of the Lord.

Binsey Poplars

MY aspens dear, whose airy cages quelled,
Quelled or quenched in leaves the leaping sun,
All felled, felled, are all felled;
 Of a fresh and following folded rank
  Not spared, not one
  That dandled a sandalled
  Shadow that swam or sank
On meadow and river and wind-wandering
 weed-winding bank.

 O if we but knew what we do
  When we delve or hew—
 Hack and rack the growing green!
  Since country is so tender
 To touch, her being só slender,
 That, like this sleek and seeing ball
 But a prick will make no eye at all,

 Where we, even where we mean
  To mend her we end her,
  When we hew or delve:
After-comers cannot guess the beauty been.
 Ten or twelve, only ten or twelve
  Strokes of havoc únselve
  The sweet especial scene,
 Rural scene, a rural scene,
 Sweet especial rural scene.

· · · · · · ·

• 71

An Oxford poem, dated 13 March 1879. Even in so ecologically minded an age as the early twenty-first century, the
opening, considered as an apostrophe of trees, is somewhat
startling: "My aspens dear". Such spontaneous "impersonation" of natural organisms (to be distinguished from "personification", which implies a "conscious act of intellectual
reasoning")[72] raises the question of Hopkins's attitude to
nature with peculiar force. In a journal entry for 1873,
Hopkins gives his reaction to tree-felling at Manresa House:

> The ashtree . . . was lopped first: I heard the sound and see
> ing it maimed there came at that moment a great pang and
> I wished to die and not see the inscapes of the world
> destroyed any more.[73]

The extremity of the feeling justifies Dr Patricia Ball when
she writes:

> All the intensity which the Romantics brought to the study
> of personal identity, Hopkins inherits, and it goes into his
> concept of inscape. He needs a term to convey the results of
> his experience of objects, for this amounts to no less than a
> revelation of their self being, that 'individual essence' or
> unique impression of an active identity which goes far
> beyond a merely accurate itemizing of appearance.[74]

Hopkins's goal was to "read" the thing in its "full design"
(Ball's words), or what W. H. Gardner called its "delicate
and surprising uniqueness".[75] Achieving that goal meant

---

72 W. A. M. Peters, SJ, *Gerard Manley Hopkins,* 8.
73 *Journals,* 230.
74 P. A. Ball, *The Science of Aspects. The Changing Role of Fact in the
   Work of Coleridge, Ruskin and Hopkins* (London 1971), 107.
75 W. H. Gardner, "Introduction", in idem, (ed.), *Poems and Prose
   of G. M. Hopkins* (Oxford 1953), xxi.

for him not only understanding but love for the object so revealed. "As soon as an object was perceived as 'charged with love, charged with God', and thereby began to [as Hopkins would put it in "As kingfishers catch fire"] deal out its own being . . . , it consequently affected other beings that became the object of this activity"[76]—and here, in the case of the Binsey poplars, Hopkins himself. The created universe in which we live is typified, for Hopkins, by ceaseless exchange, reciprocal affecting, intercommunion. This is what one would expect if created being derives from an uncreated Source which preeminently bears these qualities as the divine Trinity.

The poplars that concerned Hopkins had lined the Thames going upriver from Oxford's Medley Weir toward Godstow. Among Oxford undergraduates in the late 1960s (when the present writer was one), this was a favourite walk owing not least to the charm of "The Trout" inn and the excellence of its beer. More exactly, the trees were—as Hopkins's opening words tell us—aspens, a species belonging to the willow family and called botanically *Populus tremula* owing to the curious way their leaves tremble or shiver. They are not a long-lived tree, rarely surviving more than fifty years.[77] (Hopkins may not have not been aware of that or had his own reasons for discounting it.) He made the discovery that the tall, pole-like trees had been cut down on the afternoon of the day the poem was written. Its first two lines turn on a powerful image: the straight trunks of the

---

76 W. A. M. Peter, SJ, *Gerard Manley Hopkins,* 133. Peters points out how some of Hopkins's stranger verbal forms and inversions of normal word order are intended to bring out this subject-affecting "activity".

77 R. Mabey, *Flora Britannica,* 138. This superbly encyclopaedic work cites at this point the first four and a half lines of Hopkins's poem.

trees are as it were the bars of a cage where the setting sun is, beast-like, "quelled" by its captivity, its light "quenched in leaves": leaves just attaining their first post-winter fullness at the time that the labourers' axes were brought to bear. Read with the stresses Hopkins intended for the thrice repeated "felled", we are meant to hear the blows of the hatchets as they hit their target. The ever resourceful Norman MacKenzie notes the way Hopkins reverses the direction of a Homeric simile. In his epics Homer compares warriors toppled in battle to great trees falling. For Hopkins, the sturdy line of the young trees, drawn up army style in a "fresh and following folded rank", have been cut down by their enemy, "Not spared, not one". "Dandling" their "sandalled" feet in the water, as they used to, may seem to interrupt the military image. But Roman soldiers wore sandals, and the image is not so much roughly curtailed as subtly transformed when we are asked to imagine the fretwork of the branches casting its dancing shadow as the sunlight plays on the river water, the overgrown "weed-winding" bank, and the adjacent meadowland.

Hopkins's response, even more devastating than his earlier half-wish that he were dead, if more obliquely expressed, is to think in this connexion of the Crucifixion of Christ. Among the last words from the Cross were "Father, forgive them, for they know not what they do" (Luke 23:34). Hopkins picks up these words when he in turn cries: "O if we but knew what we do when we delve or hew". It is not that Christ is suffering in the trees, but that his creative presence in nature is thwarted by examples of the human destructiveness that *did* require his all-redemptive Passion. His spiritual notes give us the theological background, expressed in a characteristically Scotist fashion:

Had there been no sin of angels or men, the coming of
Christ would have been the efflorescence or natural consummation of the creative strain; men's minds and wills
would have risen spontaneously and harmoniously from
creatures to God. But, as a result of sin, natural values went
astray and Christ had to perform a violent readjustment of
them by his redemptive suffering. The redemptive strain
still continues the creative strain.[78]

Hopkins may have been tempted to a doctrinally overwrought deduction by knowledge of the legend that the
aspen tree trembles because from its wood was made the
instrument of the crucifixion of Christ. On the other hand,
he experienced man's hacking and racking of nature as not
only a personal injury but a Christological affront to the
One through whom all things are made. And nature's being
is "só slender" that man can extinguish it (in various of its
representatives) as easily as sight can be extinguished by the
thrusting into the eye of a bare bodkin. Even with the best
of intentions—not that these are always present—in the
attempt to "mend her we end her". Posterity is the loser. A
dozen axe-strikes' "strokes of havoc"—can, as here, "únselve"
the "sweet especial rural scene". We recall that for Hopkins
"inscape" ' can be found in natural scenes and not simply, as
with Scotus' "haecceities", in natural objects. It is always the
expression of "instress", which here means divine agency.
Ruskin had written in the first volume of *Modern Painters*
"the Divine mind is . . . visible in its full energy of operation
on every lowly bank".[79] Snuffing out an opportunity for its

---

78 *Sermons,* 290.
79 Cited in A. Ball, *The Science of Aspects,* 101.

self-expression is ontological diminution which also dimin-
ishes me.[80]

---

[80] By coincidence, it was Ruskin's sight of a "small aspen tree against
the blue sky" at Fontainebleau in 1842 which, according to his
autobiography, *Praeterita,* finally revealed to him neglected possibilities in the loving observation of nature: thus ibid., 58. Ball
explains how for Ruskin "Seeing clearly . . . means reading deeply
into the object, recognising the comprehensiveness of its self-
expression, as it demonstrates its energies, displays the formal laws
of its being, and sums up its past and its potential simply by the
impact of its visual presence", ibid., 69. All of that is highly appli-
cable to "Binsey Poplars".

Duns Scotus's Oxford

TOWERY city and branchy between towers;
Cuckoo-echoing, bell-swarmèd, lark-charmèd, rook-racked,
    river-rounded;
The dapple-eared lily below thee; that country and town did
Once encounter in, here coped and poisèd powers;

Thou hast a base and brickish skirt there, sours
That neighbour-nature thy grey beauty is grounded
Best in; graceless growth, thou hast confounded
Rural rural keeping—folk, flocks, and flowers.

Yet ah! this air I gather and I release
He lived on; these weeds and waters, these walls are what
He haunted who of all men most sways my spirits to peace;

Of realty the rarest-veinèd unraveller; a not
Rivalled insight, be rival Italy or Greece;
Who fired France for Mary without spot.

·   ·   ·   ·   ·   ·   ·

This is a poem written at Oxford itself, in the March of
either 1878 or 1879. When Hopkins was an undergraduate, mid-Victorian Oxford was already expanding, not least
through the commissioning of new buildings by the colleges. But its atmosphere was closer to the Oxford of the
eighteenth century than it soon became. The two parts of
the sonnet's sestet suggest how Hopkins, by the time of his

pastorate—scarcely more than ten years later—had noticed an unpleasing difference. The opening lines, in praise of the "towery city", conjure up an idyllic scene. As one of Hopkins's biographers has written:

> Dusty trees still lined the mostly unpaved lanes, . . . and the gowns and robes of undergraduates and senior members of the University out of their colleges gave the drowsy streets the look of aquatints. The 'river-rounded' little city was almost as self-contained physically as it had been when its limits were set by medieval walls. True, the countryside no longer lapped up to the grey stone of the colleges, but the city was distinctly marked out like an understated English Carcassonne, its perimeter uninsistently guarded on three sides by the Thames and its tributaries, to be crossed only by toll bridges.[81]

Hopkins portrays the city's appearance as a delightful synthesis of trees and towers, nature and human civilization harmoniously combining: "Towery . . . and branchy between towers". This is *rus in urbe*, "country in city", a classical ideal for the proper setting of human living. If there is noise pollution it is of an acceptable kind: the city is "bell-swarmèd" and "rook-racked", both of which sound a little grating, as well as "cuckoo-echoing" and "lark-charmèd", entirely positive descriptions. These were both birds for which Hopkins had an affection.[82] On the edges of the city grew the "dapple-eared lily"—a wealth of variegated wild orchises are still (2005) to be seen in the fields across the Thames from Christ Church Meadow. As usual, Hopkins prefers to self-coloured

---

81 R. B. Martin, *Gerard Manley Hopkins,* 25.
82 For the cuckoo, see above, "The May Magnificat"; the lark is praised in two sonnets from Hopkins's years at St Beuno's, "The Sea and the Skylark" and "The Caged Skylark".

creatures those that manifest "dapple", which gives more tes-
timony to the intrinsic and ever surprising variedness of creation. But the *rus in urbe* is threatened by the intervention of
tedious suburbs. Once the "encounter" of country and town
loses immediacy, something happens, Hopkins thinks, to
human powers, to our attitudes and capacities.

The remaining lines of the octet are distinctly bad-tem-
pered, and all too prophetic of the imminent future. R. B.
Martin notes that the coming of the railway to Oxford
(much fought over by the dons) was

> symbolic of the industrialization that was to overwhelm
> this most romantic of English cities and that was to gobble
> up much of the countryside that Hopkins feared for.[83]

Lecturing at Oxford in 1872, and so midway between
Hopkins's periods of residence, Ruskin declared that to
redeem the city visually it would be necessary to undo the
greater part of the building schemes of the previous two
decades. The loveliest approach to the city of any university
town in Europe had been turned into a "wilderness of
obscure and base buildings". This was Hopkins's point, and
his own lament for "the base and brickish skirt" picks up at
least one of Ruskin's adjectives.[84]

In the sestet he takes consolation from the figure of
Duns Scotus: his fellow Englishman (so it was widely
believed in contemporary scholarship) and Catholic religious, like Hopkins, Oxford-trained and a notable devotee
of the Virgin. The awareness that he breathes the "same" air
as Scotus gives him relief. "Yet ah! this air I gather and
release / He lived on". Scotus had been at Merton College,

---

[83] R. B. Martin, *Gerard Manley Hopkins,* 25.
[84] Cited from J. Ruskin, *The Eagle's Nest,* in N. H. MacKenzie, *A
Reader's Guide to Gerard Manley Hopkins,* 112.

whose southern perimeter walls abutted on Christ Church Meadow, which itself runs down to the river below Folly Bridge. This is probably the vantage-point, whether real or imagined, for Hopkins's poem. Here the "weeds and the water" were undeniably still present, as they had been in the fourteenth century, and Hopkins would no doubt have been aware that a percentage at least of the walls visible from the spot—such as Merton Chapel, and some of the former St Frideswide's collegiate church (after the Reformation, Christ Church cathedral)—dated to at least Scotus's time. Hence "these walls" were medieval masonry Scotus himself saw and could have touched. They were "what / He haunted", the philosopher-theologian "who of all men most sways my spirit to peace".

This is high praise, and given the austerely technical character of most of Scotus's writing (he is one of the most difficult of the high scholastics to read), we may wonder what Hopkins means. The principal justification he gives is that Scotus was "of realty the rarest-veinèd unraveller": in other words, Scotus is outstanding for his explorations of ontology, the philosophy of being. No thinker, whether "of Italy" or "of Greece", can match him, on Hopkins's view. Greece is the home of ontological thought, which is a discovery of the ancient Hellenes. But the classical Roman civilization was in philosophical matters a culture of epigones, whose work was derivative from the Greek thinkers. When he wrote "of Italy" Hopkins probably had in mind St Thomas Aquinas, born in the Kingdom of Naples of Lombard parentage. This is an affirmation, then, of his preference for Blessed John— as Scotus became in the pontificate of John Paul II—over against St Thomas. What Hopkins took from Scotus's ontology was above all a confirmation of the importance of "inscape"—which, as the Introduction to this commentary recalls, is fundamental to his view of natural objects (if not only of them).

For Scotus "haecceities"—"thisnesses", which he deemed to be non-qualitative properties, are vital for explaining not only the distinction between individual things but also their non-instantiability. (In a modern example, a clone of a cat is not an instance of the original cat but of feline nature.) Scotus holds that haecceities, like essences, are (distinct) real properties of substances, key metaphysical constituents of them. What Scotus is most assuredly *not* is any kind of Nominalist, and his ontological realism is well compared by Hopkins to that of a mining engineer investigating ("unravelling") the real properties of ore-bearing rocks. Commonalities (natures) are real—here Scotus develops what is already given in Aquinas's little treatise on ontology, the *De ente et essentia*, but goes beyond it by ascribing existence to a nature *even as abstracted from the particulars into which it is divided.* Such abstraction is of course a logical process, not a chronological one. Scotus is not saying natures exist before there are any examples of them. But equally evidently, Scotus would reject the view that individuality is everything. Yet even before he coined the term "haecceity" Scotus is insistent on a strong account of the individuality of any given particular, an account, most notably, which will explain its indivisibility as well. Haecceities, as Dr Richard Cross puts it, "tie such [common] natures to individuals" and hence "must be equally real too".[85] Though Scotus sometimes calls a haecceity a form— it would be then *individual form*—its status as form in his writing is actually uncertain since, he insists, a "thisness"

---

[85] R. Cross, "Medieval Theories of Haecceity", in E. N. Zalla (ed.), *The Stanford Encyclopaedia of Philosophy* (Stanford, CA 1995) [electronic resource], sub loc.

lacks all correspondence to any conceptual content. "As irreducibly particular, it shares no real feature in common with any other thing".[86] The haecceity and the nature-in-particular are thus distinct. Scotus's view that the accidental quantities, qualities, and relations of a substance are also individuated by their own haecceities adds—perhaps unbearably—to the complexity of his metaphysics, but may also have attracted Hopkins's favourable notice. This is assuming Hopkins looked further into Scotus than the latter's Oxford *Commentary on the Sentences*—not where contemporary scholars chiefly seek enlightenment on these matters.[87]

It is perhaps with relief that the reader turns their mind to Hopkins's last line: "Who fired France for Mary without spot", which refers to a less demanding aspect of John Duns Scotus's thought. Scotus's Mariology is strongly connex with his soteriology, or doctrine of salvation. It conforms to the abundance of the divine life that God in Christ saves people in a variety of modes and degrees. But it is a demand of his perfection that at least one person should be saved in the most superlative way possible, which is to be so utterly redeemed that the evil of sin fails to touch them from the first moment of their existence. The identity of this uniquely redeemed creature is not far to seek. It is she whom the Greeks call *achrantos* and the Latins declare *sine macula*, "without a stain".

---

86 Ibid. I am grateful to Br Dominic Ryan, OP, of Blackfriars Oxford for drawing my attention to this article.

87 W. Park, "Haecceitas and the Bare Particular", *Review of Metaphysics* 44 (1990): 375–97; S. Dumont, "The Question on Individuation in Scotus's 'Quaestiones super Metaphysicam'", in L. Sileo (ed.), *Via Scoti: Methodologica ad mentem Joannis Duns Scoti. Atti del Congresso Scotistico Internazionale. Roma 9–11 Marzo 1993* (Rome 1995), I, 193–227. For the overall context of Scotus's thought, see R. Cross, *Duns Scotus* (New York and Oxford 1999).

The Blessed Virgin was saved and redeemed by Christ her son not less than others but more, for she was saved from even falling but they were let fall and then recovered (that is / redeemed): now, as the proverb says, prevention is better than cure.[88]

Was she not, then, redeemed? Why, certainly!

For redeem may be said not only of the recovering from sin to grace or perdition to salvation but also of the raising from worthlessness before God (and all creation is unworthy of God) to worthiness of him, the meriting of God himself, or, so to say, godworthiness. In this sense the Blessed Virgin was beyond all others redeemed, because it was her more than all other creatures that Christ meant to win from nothingness and it was her that he meant to raise the highest.[89]

Why does Hopkins say that Scotus fired *France* in particular for these notions? Chiefly because Scotus taught this theological doctrine in Paris, but perhaps too because devotion to the Immaculate Virgin was prominent in the France of Hopkins's own day, not least since the "appearances" of the Virgin in the (Parisian) Rue du Bac, in 1830. (Historically, the Catholic nation most devoted to the Mother of God under the title of "The Immaculate" was Spain, whose patron the *Immaculada* was. There even the Dominicans, traditionally cautious about the doctrine which would be defined as dogma in 1854, rallied to some version of the Scotist view.)

---

[88] *Sermons*, 43.
[89] Ibid.

The Candle Indoors

SOME candle clear burns somewhere I come by.
I muse at how its being puts blissful back
With yellowy moisture mild night's blear-all black
Or to-fro tender trambeams truckle at the eye.

By that window what task what fingers ply,
I plod wondering, a-wanting, just for lack
Of answer the eagerer a-wanting Jessy or Jack
There / God to aggrándise, God to glorify.—

Come you indoors, come home; your fading fire
Mend first and vital candle in close heart's vault:
You there are master, do your own desire;

What hinders? Are you beam-blind, yet to a fault
In a neighbour deft-handed? Are you that liar
And, cast by conscience out, spendsavour salt?

. . . .

A trio of "priestly" poems follows in my selection. In "The Candle Indoors", Hopkins is out of doors, ruminating on a candle burning in a window as he passes by. His first thought, fascinated as he was by light in all its different modalities, is simply of the effect on the atmosphere. The city of Oxford is sunk in "night's blear-all black", but the "yellowy moisture" of the incandescent wax presses back the environing darkness. Curiously, Hopkins calls this process "blissful", an unaccountably strong word until we remember the iconic value of light for one who saw the fulfilment of all human striving in the beatific vision whose medium is the *lumen gloriae*, the "*light* of glory". In a line singled out for its memorability by the editor of the second edition of Hopkins's poems, the novelist and lay theologian Charles Williams, himself a poet: "to-fro tender trambeams truckle at the eye". This is a more prosaic thought, insofar as it concerns light-mechanics. But at the same time it exemplifies the demands on us of Hopkins's poetic diction. Inevitably, in his study of Hopkins's language the critic James Milroy, when offering "A Commentary on Words Used in Rare, Special or Non-Standard Senses in Hopkins's Poetry", has to help readers here: both "trambeam" and "truckle" figure in his list.[90] A "tramway" is so called because smooth beams of wood are iron-plated to allow streetcars to move. But in itself "tram" means, essentially, a shaft or bar. We call rays of light "beams" by an implicit comparison with beams of wood. Light beams "trundle" by rolling along their paths, then, before striking the retina of the human eye. But Hopkins insists that the "to-fro" process involved is "tender", and to this qualifier two secondary senses of "tram" and "truckle" apply. In nineteenth century silk-making, "trams" were silk threads used for weft or cross-threading. And another sense of "truckle" in older dictionaries is to yield. MacKenzie is right, accordingly, to reach the following synthetic judgment:

> The image . . . would then be of delicate beams of light like silk threads woven by a shuttle speeding to and fro. The eye

---

[90] J. Milroy, *The Language of Gerard Manley Hopkins* (London 1977), 232–48, sub loc.

of the onlooker is held as by the tug of a light line to the bright flame.[91]

All this would be jejune were it not for the train of thinking the optical phenomenon starts in Hopkins's mind. What on earth is going on in that chamber that requires candle-light—at so unearthly an hour, in so odd a position—would seem to be the implication. Engaged on his pastoral duties, perhaps a late sick call or a summons to the side of a dying person, Hopkins is consciously the priest here as well as the poet. Whatever man or woman—"Jessy or Jack"—is inside, he hopes anxiously that the work or whatever on which they are engaged is, at any rate, for God's glory: for the *increase* of God's glory: "God to aggrándise, God to glorify". In the Gospels the Lord had compared the good works of his disciples to a lamp placed on a stand to give light to the entire house: good works that "give glory" to the Father in heaven (Matthew 5:17). So the connexion is not, for a man with a biblical culture, so obscure.

But the "turn" of the sonnet finds him having second thoughts. Charity, we are told, "begins at home". One thing that signifies is that *our own conversion* is the first requirement for us of the love of God, long before we begin to worry about anyone else's.

In a fashion it would be easy to document from the Fathers and the medieval spiritual writers, Hopkins interprets this as a summons to interiority. Go within and attend to what you find. "Come you indoors, come home". Not that out-of-doors indoors where a candle is burning in a stranger's homestead, but the "indoors" that is intimately your own. Discover the condition of your own spiritual

91 N. H. MacKenzie, *A Reader's Guide to Gerard Manley Hopkins*, 118–19.

ardour and illumination—or, as it turns out, the lack of them: "your fading fire / Mend first and vital candle in close heart's vault". The report is disquieting. On his reception of the infused virtues of faith, hope, and love, and consequent cultivation of them depends his own relation to the God of glory, since these are—for Thomas Aquinas, and subsequently, the entire catechetical tradition of Catholicism—the "theological" or God-directed virtues *in excelsis*. Jesuits and Dominicans have not agreed historically about the doctrine of grace. When Hopkins says, "You there are master, do your own desire", let us take this as a reference to the doctrine of cooperative grace which both schools have in common. Augustine had warned his congregations that the God who created them without their assistance will not save them without their cooperation. Here freedom is active, enabled and supported by grace: This is the "master[y]" for which our own "desire" is, in that gracious context, sufficient for our sanctification.

So in what remains of the sestet Hopkins finishes on an evangelical note, with a flurry of references to the teachings of Jesus in the Synoptic tradition. He remembers the warning of Jesus against those who criticise the minor faults of others but fail to attend to the grievous faults they have themselves: The man who sees the "mote" or tiny speck that is in his neighbour's eye, but not the "beam" that is in his own (Matthew 7:3; Luke 6:41). The metaphors are taken from the threshing floor. One workman squints momentarily because a tiny piece of chaff has flown into his eye. The other has his vision obstructed by a rafter. Hopkins fear that as a priest with a professional duty of moral vigilance he may himself be "beam-blind". The householder with the candle burning at all hours could simply be "deft-handed", an industrious man or woman working overtime. How deplorable if the comparable skill

Hopkins showed were only in sniffing out others' sins (not least *rather than* one's own). The Saviour, speaking roundly to the ultra-observant Pharisees, called such conduct hypocrisy, a form of lying. Hopkins turns against himself these hard sayings, meditating that, by indulging a misplaced conscientiousness, and without purification of the will in appropriate self-reform, he could be, like the salt that has lost its savour in the Gospel, thrown out of the kingdom of God (Matthew 5:13): "cast by conscience out". There is more than one way to become "spendsavour salt".

Two poems follow where we can monitor the evangelical seriousness with which Hopkins went about his sacramental ministrations: first as minister of Holy Communion, the Blessed Eucharist, and secondly of Extreme Unction, the Anointing of the Sick for the dying.

The Bugler's First Communion

A BUGLER boy from barrack (it is over the hill
There)—boy bugler, born, he tells me, of Irish
     Mother to an English sire (he
Shares their best gifts surely, fall how things will),

This very very day came down to us after a boon he on
My late being there begged of me, overflowing
     Boon in my bestowing,
Came, I say, this day to it—to a First Communion.

Here he knelt then ín regimental red.
Forth Christ from cupboard fetched, how fain I of feet
     To his youngster take his treat!
Low-latched in leaf-light housel his too huge godhead.

There! and your sweetest sendings, ah divine,
By it, heavens, befall him! as a heart Christ's darling, dauntless;
     Tongue true, vaunt- and tauntless;
Breathing bloom of a chastity in mansex fine.

Frowning and forefending angel-warder
Squander the hell-rook ranks sally to molest him;
     March, kind comrade, abreast him;
Dress his days to a dexterous and starlight order.

How it dóes my heart good, visiting at that bleak hill,
When limber liquid youth, that to all I teach
     Yields tender as a pushed peach,
Hies headstrong to its wellbeing of a self-wise self-will!

Then though I should tread tufts of consolation
Dáy áfter, só I in a sort deserve to
      And do serve God to serve to
Just such slips of soldiery Christ's royal ration.

Nothing élse is like it, no, not all so strains
Us: freshyouth fretted in a bloomfall all portending
      That sweet's sweeter ending;
Realm both Christ is heir to and thére réigns.

O now well work that sealing sacred ointment!
O for now charms, arms, what bans off bad
      And locks love ever in a lad!
Let mé though see no more him, and not disappointment

Those sweet hopes quell whose least me quickenings lift,
In scarlet or somewhere of some day seeing
      That brow and bead of being,
An our day's God's own Galahad. Though this child's drift

Seems by a dívine doom chánnelled, nor do I cry
Disaster there; but may he not rankle and roam
      In backwheels though bound home?—
That left to the Lord of the Eucharist, I here lie by;

Recorded only, I have put my lips on pleas
Would brandle adamantine heaven with ride and jar, did
      Prayer go disregarded:
Forward-like, but however, and like favourable heaven heard
      these.

·   ·   ·   ·   ·   ·   ·

Written in Oxford in late the July of 1879. Here the priestly
Hopkins gives a young soldier his first Holy Communion.
In suitable conditions—and, for a soldier on imminent call-

up such were no doubt sometimes verified—this might be done, according to the liturgical law in vigour in the Latin church in Hopkins's time, "from the tabernacle": that is, from the Reserved Sacrament kept in church for communicating the sick and for purposes of devotion, rather than—as more normal—during the celebration of the Mass. That at least appears to be the setting of this poem.

One of Hopkins's duties as a curate at St Aloysius was to serve as chaplain to the Cowley Barracks. He noted on his manuscript copy of the poem that the youth was to sail for India at the end of September, being ordered to Multan in the Punjab. Evidently his company was needed on the then-turbulent "north-west frontier" between the Raj and Afghanistan, a territory coveted by Britain chiefly to prevent its occupation by Russia during the late nineteenth-century "Great Game" of competitive diplomacy and military expansion in the Himalayan zone. This particular young man was, like many British Catholics then and since, Anglo-Irish. Hopkins, who found Ireland alien when he went to live there, is here pretty even-handed with his praise of the two ethnic stocks (Hibernian and Anglo-Saxon) involved: the soldier "shares their best gifts surely" (stanza 1). The service he sought from Hopkins, communication with the Eucharistic host, was something which in this period (as almost universally in Church history) only a priest (or a bishop) could provide. Ordination had given Hopkins a ministerial share in the High Priesthood of Christ, who at the Last Supper had instituted in advance the sacrament of his own saving sacrifice on Calvary. Hopkins notes the disparity between the gift—in Catholic doctrine the Eucharistic elements, once consecrated, are "transubstantiated, their reality that of Christ himself in his body and blood, with his soul and divinity—and the ministerial giver. Holy Communion was, he remarks, with wonder at his own—Church-mandated—

audacity, an "overflowing boon in my possession" (stanza 2).
A priest engaged Eucharistically is, as it were, dispensing
largesse from an inexhaustible bank account not a penny of
which is his own. In the practice which reigned in the Latin
rite from the high Middle Ages until the 1970s, the sacrament was given "under the form of bread", which typically
meant thin discs baked from highly refined wheaten flour. It
was thought irreverent to chew the sacred Host, so the
method of manufacture (generally by nuns) produced a substance that could more or less dissolve on the tongue. The
fragility of the elements accentuated the contrast with their
ontological weightiness, which derived from their being the
"efficacious sign" (such was the Thomistic expression) of the
real presence of the God-man. Hence Hopkins's description
of the Host he carries from the Eucharistic tabernacle to the
altar-rails: "Low-latched in leaf-light housel his [Christ's] too
huge godhead". By using the Middle English name for the
Communion wafer, the "housel", rather than the more customary Latinate word "Host", Hopkins was drawing attention to the continuity of Roman Catholicism with the
religion of the pre-Reformation English people—in which
they were united, of course, with the Irish of the same
period. The same instinct—as well as love of alliteration—
governs his avoidance of the term "tabernacle" (another word
of Latin provenance) for the sacrament house and its replacing by the humble, but undeniably English, "cupboard". It is
from there that "Christ . . . [is] fetched".

The act of the soldier's reception of Communion is sig-
nalled by a one-word exclamation: "There!" But Hopkins's
full response takes the rest of this fourth stanza and the whole
of the fifth too. Hopkins combined the intelligence of a half
a dozen professors with the piety of a first communicant, and
here we witness the sheer force of that piety, a term which
too often can seem pale and lily-livered—though not when it

makes an early appearance in the hero of the *Aeneid*, Virgil's
pius Aeneas. Hopkins positively assaults heaven with prayer
for the lad, asking the "divine . . . heavens" for their "sweetest
sendings", perhaps meaning thereby the seven Gifts of the
Holy Spirit, which are given embryonically in principle in
Confirmation, but which the grace of the Eucharist, as the
compendium of the entire sacramental life, reinvigorates
and expands. As the sun of the sacramental cosmos the
Eucharist is polyvalent in the gifts it represents, but, more
than gifts of direct divine union, Hopkins seems to have in
mind the guarding and development of the young man's
basic Christian life, especially in its dimension of moral
witness. He finds him already admirable in his fortitude as
a Catholic Christian determined on an upright and godly
life. He is "dauntless", "tongue-true", "vaunt-[less]", "taunt-
less": all of which terms suggest the youth's candour and
courage in speaking up, and standing up, for what he
believes in—not so easy in the roughhouse atmosphere of
army life for private soldiers. He is also—and this is another
triumph, not least in the circumstances—chaste, and not
owing to any lack of physical charms: "Breathing bloom of
a chastity in mansex fine" (stanza 4). That these qualities
are not merely hopeful projections for the future from the
Eucharistic graces of the present becomes apparent when
Hopkins's prayer turns from the imploring to the apotropaic.
He calls on the lad's angel guardian to defend him in his
possession, then, of what already exists. In language at once
martial and phantasmagoric (possibly he was inspired here
by the demonic choruses in Newman's *The Dream of
Gerontius*), Hopkins conjures up a picture of the demonic
enemies the angel is to engage on the boy's behalf. The
angel must "Squander the hell-rook ranks sally to molest
him". And Hopkins imagines the angelic guard acting in
appropriately military fashion by "march[ing]" to "abreast

him" as a "comrade", and "dress[ing] his days" to a suitable
order, as if on parade. In "abreast" we may also catch a
warmer, cordial note—the *heart* is in the breast, and the
"order" is not only "dexterous" (by the—moral and spiritual—right, quick march!), it is also "starlight", with all the
connotations that word carried for Hopkins of divine luminosity expressed in points of light visible on earth.

In the following stanzas, Hopkins gives voice to the
pleasure his apostolate gives him. By his own admission in
his letters, he did not find the Catholics among the Oxford
townspeople terribly sympathetic. But it was different in
the barracks, where young men, hardly more than boys, in
a culture of deference where the secularism—the vogue
term would have been the agnosticism—already common
in the intellectual elite in England had not yet seeped
through, were highly amenable to Hopkins's efforts at cate-
chesis. Their sheer docility was the first thing that capti-
vated him: they are "limber liquid youth, that to all I teach
/ Yields tender as a pushed peach". But these are not papier-
mâché people. Part of Hopkins's delight is that this suscep-
tibility to Catholic doctrine and devotion is that of youth
well-endowed with natural assertiveness, that "hies headstrong to its wellbeing of a self-wise self-will" (stanza 6).
That of course makes the victory of grace the more remarkable. Hopkins finds himself treading "tufts of consolation",
as though walking on the springy sea-coast grass that both
cushions one's step and by its resilience prompts one forward. Serving these "slips of solidery" with the Eucharistic
Bread, "Christ's royal ration", a right royal feast on him
who is not only a king but the King of kings: this really is
at the same time serving God as well (stanza 7).

Nothing so moves him to priestly fervour than these ministrations to "freshyouth", since, as Donald McChesney help-
fully comments about the difficult eighth stanza of the poem,

"the sight of such bloom and freshness is a symbol of 'that sweet's sweeter ending', the Paradise of Heaven", the "realm" which "Christ is heir to" and indeed already "thére réigns".[92]

In the remaining stanzas, the poet steps back to survey the wider saving economy in which his soldier-charge is involved, and his own hopes and fears for him in the wider context of human life on which that economy must set to work. His prayer that "the sealing sacred ointment" may "well work" in the lad (stanza 9) seems to be a request—along the lines of the interpretation I offered of the fourth stanza—that the grace of Confirmation, the sacrament whose "matter" is the oil of chrism, will be reactualised by his Eucharistic participation. This he must leave to "the Lord of the Eucharist", because who knows what spiritual ill future corrupting influences will produce, possibly annulling, or even reversing, the advance in grace a devout sacramental Communion represents? The young man's drift—the fundamental direction of his life—seems set by grace, "by a dívine doom chánnelled", and it may not be presumptuous then to call him an "our day's God's own Galahad" (stanza 10), a very perfect gentle Christian knight. But despite the sufficient grace he has received, which should carry him "home" to the *patria* of our pilgrimage, there is no guarantee, Hopkins reminds us, that he will not "rankle and roam / In backwheels" (stanza 11). Catholic doctrine has no version of the Calvinist "amissibility of salvation", the grace of final perseverance must always be prayed for. That is why, all things considered, Hopkins would prefer not to meet the young soldier again, just in case life makes of so promising a disciple of Christ a spiritual casualty after all. Lest that seem a defeatist ending, Hopkins promises he will storm heaven and shake its battlements, "brandle" it with "ride and jar", for the

---

[92] D. McChesney, *A Hopkins Commentary*, 100.

man's soul (stanza 12). The syntax of the last line almost
defies unravelling but indicates how Hopkins admits his
worries are premature ("forward-like") and probably ("like")
heaven will see the boy through.

Hopkins has shocked the readers of his letters by admit-
ting to Bridges that he half-hoped the subject of this poem
would be killed in the Afghan wars—rather than survive
and lapse from the faith.[93] McChesney points out that
Hopkins's apparently life-denying, idealistic other-worldli-
ness here looks rather different—and certainly more interesting—when viewed in the perspective of three theological
convictions.[94] And these are: first, that "the lost kingdom
of innocence still lies in our hearts and can occasionally be
seen in the face of youth"; secondly, that "to such a world
of innocence, if man had not fallen, Christ would have
come, not as a poor man to be crucified, but in his true
splendour as King and High Priest";[95] thirdly, that "all bap-
tized and confirmed Christians are 'knights' of Christ, 'and
having been knighted are bound by allegiance, fealty, loy-
alty, chivalry' ".[96]

---

[93] *Letters,* 92.
[94] D. McChesney, *A Hopkins Commentary,* 97–98.
[95] That is a Scotist thesis: See *Sermons,* 6.
[96] Ibid., 163.

Felix Randal

FELIX RANDAL the farrier, O is he dead then? my duty all
      ended,
Who have watched his mould of man, big-boned and hardy-
      handsome
Pining, pining, till time when reason rambled in it and some
Fatal four disorders, fleshed there, all contended?

Sickness broke him. Impatient, he cursed at first, but mended
Being anointed and all; though a heavenlier heart began some
Months earlier, since I had our sweet reprieve and ransom
Tendered to him. Ah well, God rest him all road ever he
      offended!

This seeing the sick endears them to us, us too it endears.
My tongue had taught thee comfort, touch had quenched thy
      tears,
Thy tears that touched my heart, child, Felix, poor Felix Randal;

How far from then forethought of, all thy more boisterous
      years,
When thou at the random grim forge, powerful amidst peers,
Didst fettle for the great grey drayhorse his bright and battering
      sandal!

.   .   .   .

This is a Liverpool poem, dated 28 April 1880, and includes
touches of Lancashire dialect such as "all road" for "always".
Once again it shows Hopkins in his pastoral mode, as the

priest, this time, of the Anointing of the Sick. "Felix Randal" is a part pseudonym for one of Hopkins's parishioners, Felix Spencer. The name "Felix" means "happy", and possibly the poet retained it, despite its clue to identity, because it was an element in his message that this poor man, who tried tragically young, was indeed, in an unconventional sense of the word, "happy" at the end. "Randal" is, we hear, a farrier: that is, a blacksmith, an important craft at a time when the overland conveyance of goods in industrial south Lancashire was done by teams of drayhorses. As the commentators point out, only very strong, fit men could handle these gigantic horses since the process of shoeing entails gripping and lifting their legs, and often allowing the horse to rest some of its body-weight against the smith at the same time. Much of the force of the poem turns on the contrast between the remembrance of past virility and stunning health and the state to which Felix is now reduced.

Hopkins had evidently visited him regularly during his rapid decline (apparently from tuberculosis with complications), and preached the homily at his Requiem. Now his "duty" was "all ended", unless we can regard the writing of the poem as itself an act of priestly charity, disengaging and celebrating, however soberly, the meaning of Felix's life. The slightly built Hopkins admired the farrier's "mould": "big-boned and hardy-handsome", and its gradual collapse with "fatal four disorders, fleshed there", was as distressing to him as the mental disintegration which seemed to be accompanying it when, under the impact of his physical condition, the patient rambled.

The second and third stanzas record the alleviating, even sweetening, effect of Hopkins's sacramental care and pastoral counsel to the terminally ill man, who at thirty-two was only four years younger than Hopkins was himself. At first Felix had reacted to the illness by imprecations. Hopkins goes so far as to write, "Sickness broke him". But a change in spiritual outlook had set in. Hopkins identifies three means that brought it about. First, as with the bugler, he had brought the man Holy Communion, "our sweet reprieve and ransom". Hopkins uses, with full theological legitimacy, terms from the doctrine of Christ's atoning work on the Cross. Just as the full satisfaction the God-man made there for the sins of all mankind "reprieved" those condemned to spiritual death (ourselves), and "ransomed" those who were slaves to the powers of sin and death, so the sacramental fruit of that Sacrifice, being itself Jesus Christ, the Victim offered and accepted, may be hailed by the same titles as the Crucified on Calvary. But Hopkins dates Felix's real spiritual "mending" to the administration of the Sacrament of the Sick, at this period rarely given save *in extremis*. We catch the tones of Felix's own voice when Hopkins calls it "Being anointed and all" (another Lancastrianism). And then finally, Hopkins had found, it seems, the right words of comfort and encouragement, drying the man's tears and touching his heart, though the process was mutual: Hopkins himself was deeply affected too. "This seeing the sick endears them to us, us too it endears."

It is the final tercet of the poem that has been most admired. In a spirit utterly free of all morbidity, Hopkins conjures up Felix's "boisterous years", which were totally lacking in any "forethought" of future doom. The farrier stood "powerful among peers": There is a suggestion of how he actually outstripped them in physical strength. So things were in the "random grim forge", where, presumably, tools were lying about anyhow for the blacksmith to pick carelessly as he wanted them, in a setting where the smithy's grime and fiery heat (the word "grim" serves for both) never gave him pause. In the action that sums up Randal's working life, he fixed (Hopkins uses a dialect word, "fettle") for the "great grey drayhorse" his shoe. In the verbal formula he finds for the too commonplace word "shoe"—"his bright and battering sandal", Hopkins not only ends the sonnet with a magnificent pen picture of the mighty horse stamping the ground with such force as to dent it. More than this, the "brightness" of this sandal Felix nails on conveys a sense of the smith's almost godlike powers of repairing the world in an effulgence of flame. The hint that Felix Randal is a kind of Vulcan figure (Vulcan was the Roman god of furnaces) leaves the reader with a sense that all this energy cannot be in every sense extinguished. "Sandal" is an archaic word for a type of horseshoe. But it also rhymes with "Randal".

As kingfishers catch fire

AS kingfishers catch fire, dragonflies draw flame;
  As tumbled over rim in roundy wells
  Stones ring; like each tucked string tells, each hung bell's
Bow swung finds tongue to fling out broad its name;
Each mortal thing does one thing and the same:
  Deals out that being indoors each one dwells;
  Selves—goes itself; *myself* it speaks and spells,
Crying *What I do is me: for that I came.*

Í say more: the just man justices;
  Keeps gráce: thát keeps all his goings graces;
Acts in God's eye what in God's eye he is—
  Chríst. For Christ plays in ten thousand places,
Lovely in limbs, and lovely in eyes not his
  To the Father through the features of men's faces.

. . . .

The date of writing of this poem is controverted. It has generally been placed in 1881 when, in the autumn after leaving
Liverpool and suffering a short spell in Glasgow, Hopkins
returned to Manresa for his tertianship. But close comparison of the way Hopkins gradually modified the physical lay-
out of his sonnets would lead some to locate it in the St
Beuno's period, where poems that in any case most resemble
it—notably "The Windhover" and "Hurrahing in Harvest"—belong. But a comparison with those sonnets also

suggests a difference. This is by far the most metaphysically explicit of Hopkins's poems. It is ontology as lyric.

The opening line of the octet features an aspect of the specific form of Britain's most splendid bird and insect respectively. The kingfisher, in the words of one ornithologist, is "so brightly coloured as almost to dazzle the eye in certain lights", the vivid blue plumage of its upper parts making it look, when on the wing, "like a bright blue light rather than anything solid".[97] Kingfishers certainly seem to "catch fire", then, from the sun. Britain has over forty species of dragonfly, but their common feature is to "attract even the casual observer by their brilliant colourings, [and] their glistening wings", as well as the "strong purposeful flight of the larger kinds".[98] Here again it is not hard to see how Hopkins can describe these insects as "draw[ing] flame". This sonnet is sometimes said to be the most obviously Scotist of Hopkins's poems. If so, that would not be so much here, which is an account of natural *kinds*, as in the succeeding two lines of the octet, where he puts forward an audacious account of the individuality of stones, tied in some way to one of the three competing theories of language held by late Victorian philologists.

Hopkins imagines someone throwing stones into a dried-up well. Each stone (he implicitly claims) rings in such a way as to announce its own individuality. Every "tucked string"—all the tuned strings of a musical instrument such as the violin or harp—has a definite pitch. Every bell hanging in a belfry, when it has been properly cast, makes a sound distinguishable from other bells as its "bow"—the thickened metal edge—finds the clapper or "tongue" in swinging. Each bell sings out its "name". Now

---

[97] S. Vere Benson, *The Observer's Book of Birds* (London 1956), 110.
[98] J. Clegg, *The Observer's Book of Pond Life* (London 1956), 65.

bellmakers commonly give great bells names at the behest
of their patrons (Hopkins would have been familiar with
"Great Tom", for instance, at Christ Church, Oxford). But
there is probably more at stake. First, in this insistence on
the interrelation of ringing and naming, Hopkins's words
conjure up a contemporary debate on language.[99] At this
time in interested circles in England one could take one's
pick between the "interjectional theory" of the origin of
language (for which language begins in cries reflecting various emotional states), stigmatised by the great Victorian
philologist Max Müller as the "Pooh-pooh" theory, and the
onomatopoeic theory, based on echoism and sound-sym-
bolism, decried by Müller as the "Bow-wow" theory. Or
again one could embrace Müller's own account, which,
lambasted by others as the "Ding-dong" theory, centres on
percussiveness, while issuing a somewhat hyperbolic claim
for the continuity of language with nature. In a passage
which appears closely relevant to Hopkins's evocation of
stone on well, and ring of bell, Müller claimed:

> There is a law which runs through nearly the whole of
> nature, that everything which is struck rings. Each sub-
> stance has its peculiar ring. We can tell the more or less per-
> fect structure of metals by their vibrations, by the answer
> which they give. Gold rings differently from tin, wood rings
> differently from stone; and different sounds are produced
> according to the nature of each percussion. [So far, so good,
> but then he continues] It was the same with man, the most
> highly organized of nature's works. Man, in his primitive
> and perfect state . . . possessed . . . the faculty of giving
> more articulate expression to the rational conceptions of his

---

[99] I follow here J. Milroy, *The Language of Gerard Manley Hopkins*,
33–69.

mind. . . . So far as language is the product of that instinct, it belongs to the realm of nature.[100]

It is easy to see how Hopkins, already attracted to the ono-matopoeic theory owing to the way it justified his own belief that similarities in sound between words are also associations of meaning, could be seduced into dalliance with the percussive theory, which alone of the three seemed fully to justify the expansion of *inscape* to cover both natural things and speech. Hopkins mentions in his diary for the late summer/early autumn of 1864 that he intends to read Müller. That would most likely mean the *Lectures on the Science of Language* published in June 1864 after a highly successful oral delivery which, among other things, gained its author an invitation to sketch out his ideas to the British royal family at Osborne House.[101]

But the emphasis on the way things have their own "names" may also be a metaphorical expression of Scotist ontology: The "names" are, more properly, signs for *haecceitas*. In the second quatrain of the sonnet's sestet we find "Each mortal thing does one thing and the same". It externalises its own being, not simply as nature but as individualised selfhood or what the Thomist scholastics would call *suppositum*, the Latin equivalent of the Greek *hypostasis*, which originally meant not simply personal subjects but every single subject of a nature, whether impersonal or not. Each things "speaks and spells", says Hopkins, "*myself*", italicising so as to indicate he is "quoting" its "utterance". It "deals out" its own being, externalising what it intrinsically is within, "that being indoors each one dwells". Here all being is communicative, a truth which in the Thomism

[100] M. Müller, *Lectures on the Science of Language* (London 1864), II., 70–71.
[101] J. Milroy, *The Language of Gerard Manley Hopkins*, 50.

Hopkins had studied at Stonyhurst is expressed by the language of *form*. Curiously, as we noted when considering *Duns Scotus's Oxford*, Scotus did not think haecceities, strictly speaking, had forms since to them no conceptually articulable content belongs. But in Hopkins's revision of Scotism, if that is what it is, some articulable content most certainly belongs if each *individuality*—and not just the *nature* ontologically bonded therewith—enables a thing to cry out, *"What I do is me: for that I came"*. It is surprising that Hopkins did not incorporate in the sonnet the word "sake", which, as he explained to Bridges,

> is a word I find it convenient to use. . . . I mean by it the being a thing has outside itself, as a voice by its echo, a face by its reflection, a body by its shadow . . . *and also* that in the thing by virtue of which especially it has this being abroad, and that is something distinctive, marked, specifically or individually speaking.[102]

But even without that word, the overall context provided by the sonnet's first eight lines strongly indicates Hopkins has gone beyond the Thomistic adage that *agere sequitur esse*, "action follows on being", when the "act of existence"—the ontological root of every being in Thomas's metaphysics—is received by some essence, whose nature defines the sort of activity which will energetically follow. In his sermons, Hopkins describes how non-personal creatures fulfil their destiny and give God glory—in a "dull" way yet continuously—simply by doing what it is their nature to be. "What they can they always do".[103] But here in "As kingfishers catch fire" he really does seem to go beyond that common metaphysic of the Catholic tradition to reach a stronger statement.

---

[102] *Letters*, 83.
[103] *Sermons*, 239.

But the sonnet now reaches its "turn", where Hopkins will apply these ideas to the human creature—in which context their inadequacy immediately strikes him because no account has yet been taken of the *Christological* matrix and destiny of the world, which is found in and through man. Something more must be said, or, avoiding bureaucratese, and striking the *individually* personal note which the octet demands, as Hopkins begins: "Í say more". And the "more" is the engracing of God's human creature by justification, which, in the Catholic doctrine defined at the Council of Trent, is both the gift of God and, once given—and until and unless surrendered—the inherent received possession of man. By virtue of the grace of justification, the perfect charity of Christ is not merely "imputed" to me, by the legal legerdemain of a merciful yet distant God. Rather, while it is indeed first of all a Word of divine forgiveness that, for no virtue of mine, declares me acquitted, it also comes to dwell in me as my very own righteousness. Justification, wherever it continues to be, is always a gift, and is only for me on those terms. And yet, as the gift that it is, it constitutes a genuine grafting of the grace of Christ into my being. Or in Hopkins's words: "the just man justices; / Keeps gráce".

And that, as he explains, "keeps all his goings graces". In one of his sermons, Hopkins told the faithful:

> When a man is in God's grace and free from mortal sin, then everything that he does, so long as there is no sin in it, gives God glory. . . . To lift up the hands in prayer gives God glory, but a man with a dungfork in his hand, a woman with a sloppail, give him glory too.[104]

---

[104] Ibid., 240–41.

Man "Acts in God's eye what in God's eye he is— / Chríst".

In this quintessential doing-word "Acts", the notion of moral and spiritual agency is primary, and derives from St Paul's doctrine of the "Mystical Body", whereby the members, when they act in virtue of their justification and sanctification through baptismal faith and charity, act inseparably with their Head. But then Hopkins contributes another theme, which is that of the dramatic playing of Christ the protagonist in his troupe of actors: "for Christ plays in ten thousand places" where he is "Lovely in limbs, and lovely in eyes not his". And this seems not so much a retrospective allusion to the apostle as a prospective anticipation of the "theodramatics" of Hans Urs von Balthasar. What Hopkins has in mind is what Balthasar calls "the inclusion of the theodramatic characters in Christ".[105] As this drama plays itself out in human lives, Christ himself "plays . . . / To the Father": All is still governed by the doxological principle that glory goes to God, and ultimately to the "Principle without a principle", the Father who is the source not only of the world, and of human life within it, but of the entire divine Trinity. The astounding Incarnationalism of Hopkins's theological outlook comes home to us when we realise, thanks to the sonnet's final words, how this revelation of the Godhead through Christ in the justified takes place "through the features of men's faces". This would be a good place from which to contemplate Hopkins's concern with the saints.

---

[105] H. U. von Balthasar, *Theo-Drama. Theological Dramatic Theory. III. The Dramatis Personae: The Person in Christ*, English translation (San Francisco 1992), 55.

The Blessed Virgin compared to the Air we Breathe

WILD air, world-mothering air,
Nestling me everywhere,
That each eyelash or hair
Girdles; goes home betwixt
The fleeciest, frailest-flixed
Snowflake; that's fairly mixed
With, riddles, and is rife
In every least thing's life;
This needful, never spent,
And nursing element;
My more than meat and drink,
My meal at every wink;
This air, which, by life's law,
My lung must draw and draw
Now but to breathe its praise,
Minds me in many ways
Of her who not only
Gave God's infinity
Dwindled to infancy
Welcome in womb and breast,
Birth, milk, and all the rest
But mothers each new grace
That does now reach our race—
Mary Immaculate,
Merely a woman, yet
Whose presence, power is
Great as no goddess's

Was deemèd, dreamèd; who
This one work has to do—
Let all God's glory through,
God's glory which would go
Through her and from her flow
Off, and no way but so.
    I say that we are wound
With mercy round and round
As if with air: the same
Is Mary, more by name.
She, wild web, wondrous robe,
Mantles the guilty globe,
Since God has let dispense
Her prayers his providence:
Nay, more than almoner,
The sweet alms' self is her
And men are meant to share
Her life as life does air.
    If I have understood,
She holds high motherhood
Towards all our ghostly good
And plays in grace her part
About man's beating heart,
Laying, like air's fine flood,
The deathdance in his blood;
Yet no part but what will
Be Christ our Saviour still.
Of her flesh he took flesh:
He does take fresh and fresh,
Though much the mystery how,
Now flesh but spirit now
And makes, O marvellous!
New Nazareths in us,
Where she shall yet conceive
Him, morning, noon, and eve;
New Bethlems, and he born

There, evening, noon, and morn—
Bethlem or Nazareth,
Men here may draw like breath
More Christ and baffle death;
Who, born so, comes to be
New self and nobler me
In each one and each one
More makes, when all is done,
Both God's and Mary's Son.
    Again, look overhead
How air is azurèd;
O how! Nay do but stand
Where you can lift your hand
Skywards: rich, rich it laps
Round the four fingergaps.
Yet such a sapphire-shot,
Charged, steepèd sky will not
Stain light. Yea, mark you this:
It does no prejudice.
The glass-blue days are those
When every colour glows,
Each shape and shadow shows.
Blue be it: this blue heaven
The seven or seven times seven
Hued sunbeam will transmit
Perfect, not alter it.
Or if there does some soft,
On things aloof, aloft,
Bloom breathe, that one breath more
Earth is the fairer for.
Whereas did air not make
This bath of blue and slake
His fire, the sun would shake,
A blear and blinding ball
With blackness bound, and all
The thick stars round him roll

Flashing like flecks of coal,
Quartz-fret, or sparks of salt,
In grimy vasty vault.
　　So God was god of old:
A mother came to mould
Those limbs like ours which are
What must make our daystar
Much dearer to mankind;
Whose glory bare would blind
Or less would win man's mind.
Through her we may see him
Made sweeter, not made dim,
And her hand leaves his light
Sifted to suit our sight.
　　Be thou then, O thou dear
Mother, my atmosphere;
My happier world, wherein
To wend and meet no sin;
Above me, round me lie
Fronting my froward eye
With sweet and scarless sky;
Stir in my ears, speak there
Of God's love, O live air,
Of patience, penance, prayer:
World-mothering air, air wild,
Wound with thee, in thee isled,
Fold home, fast fold thy child.

·　　·　　·　　·　　·　　·　　·

Written in May 1883 at Stonyhurst, this is another example of the "May offerings" to the Mother of the Lord to set beside "The May Magnificat" (above). This poem was not a great favourite of Hopkins, who probably considered its metre too unadventurous. It is written in trimeter couplets, which are quite common among the Latin hymns of the Roman Office.

But Bridges, despite his Protestantism—or Protestant agnosticism—found it admirable, rather to Hopkins's surprise. (Of
course a more doctrinally committed Protestant might not
have so well kept his literary cool.) In the third (1948) edition
of the poems, W. H. Gardner summarised the theme. In this
paean to the Blessed Virgin, Hopkins:

> says that just as the atmosphere sustains the life of man and
> tempers the power of the sun's radiation, so the immaculate
> nature of Mary is the softening, humanizing medium of
> God's glory, justice and grace. Through her the ineffable
> Godhead becomes comprehensible—sweetly attuneable to
> the limited human heart.[106]

Here Hopkins places himself square in the tradition of the
seventeenth-century "Metaphysical" poets, who delighted
to work out sustained analogies between utterly disparate
aspects of experience: in this case, the air in which our biological life functions, on the one hand, and, on the other,
the gracious intercession of the Virgin, crucial as that is—
so Hopkins maintains—to our spiritual life. Gardner's sum-
mary raises a major question of theological sensibility: in
pursuing this analogy how well has Hopkins succeeded in
avoiding the impression that the "softening, humanizing'
effect of the Mother of Jesus in her distinctive role in the
economy of salvation might actually threaten to replace, in
this regard, of the humanity of her Son?

The opening is very striking. The air to which Mary will
be compared is no gentle breeze. Rather is it "Wild air",
and the adjective is repeated twice more, once in identical if
inverted terms—"air wild", and once when the Mother of
Christ is described directly as a "wild web". Norman

---

[106] *The Poems of Gerard Manley Hopkins,* ed. W. H. Gardner (London
1948), 241.

MacKenzie points out how, in Hopkins's distinctive language use, "wild" always has some reference to the way a being expresses its own nature in (more or less consummate) freedom.[107] This air—which so far is simply the physical atmosphere of planet Earth—is, Hopkins continues, "world-mothering air". No life is possible without the atmosphere that surrounds the planet. Hence all the complexly interrelated organisms which compose our world may be said to have their nurture in this element. Hopkins draws our attention to the exquisite delicacy with which the air enters our physical environment, so gently and unremarkably that I am almost always unaware of the atmosphere around me: "Nestling me everywhere", girdling "each eyelash or hair". In the outdoors cold (in the Pennines there could still be snow in early May) the air "goes home betwixt / The fleeciest, frailest-flixed [fluff-like] / Snowflake", nor is this anything unusual for it "is rife / In every least thing's life". Hopkins has now positioned himself so as to be able to explain the "world-mothering" accolade with which he began. Manifestly, the air is "This needful, never spent, / And nursing element". One would look odd without it: "This air, which by life's law / My lung must draw and draw". And now, says the poet, he is drawing it so as to sing air's praise.

Just the point at which to introduce the comparison with Mary: Hopkins characterises this other mother by two features of her role as Catholic Christianity sees it. The first is her divine motherhood, by which she became the Theotokos or God-bearer, giving welcome in "womb and breast" to the "infinity" of the person of God the Word, now become what the medievals called *Verbum abbreviatum*, the

---

107 N. H. MacKenzie, *A Reader's Guide to Gerard Manley Hopkins*, 157.

"abbreviated Word", inasmuch as his divine hypostasis, from the moment of the Annunciation onward, acts as the personalising subject of an instance of human nature. Thus is the Godhead of the Son "dwindled to infancy" in the Christ-child—without, for all that, suffering the loss of those divine attributes which make him the foundation of the universe and of the moral law. The role of our Lady at the Annunciation is so essential to Incarnation robustly conceived that it already justifies, in classical Christian vocabulary, the exalted language of channel of divine grace, which, in point of theological fact, Hopkins will use for her under a second distinct heading. Drawing on a doctrinal tradition, which has never (yet) attained dogmatic status, he affirms that she "mothers each new grace / That now does reach our race". The inclusion of the words "each new" here goes beyond what Mary's divine motherhood by itself could lead us to say; it is a confession of Mary's "sub-mediation" of the grace of Christ to individuals here and now. Were we in any doubt on the matter, Hopkins himself dispels it for us in a sermon:

> Now holiness God promotes by giving grace; the grace he gives not direct but as if stooping and drawing it from her vessel, taking it down from her storehouse and cupboard. It is in some way laid up in her.[108]

So "Mary Immaculate"—a title which had surged in popularity through the *ex cathedra* definition of the all-holiness of the Mother of God in 1854, delighting those who followed the *via Scoti*, "Scotus's way"—is "Merely a woman" and yet her "presence" and "power" is "great as no goddess's / Was deemèd, dreamèd".

---

[108] *Sermons*, 29–30.

This is a deliberately uncomfortable paradox, and Hopkins is positively willing us to ask whether he has not mired himself in contradiction. Can Mary of Nazareth, someone whose being is altogether finite (as the being of the Word incarnate is *not*), have so divine a role without calling into question her finitude or God's infinitude or both? Hopkins resolves the issue by reimagining this role as that of a pane of glass which has no more—and no less—to do that letting the Light shine through it. She "This one work has to do— / Let all God's glory through", and even this is feasible only by the divine antecedent will and covenant: "God's glory which would go / Through her and from her flow / Off, and no way but so". St Bernard, a major articulator of this tradition, remarks simply in his sermons: "It is God's will that we should receive all graces through Mary".[109]

The following lines (35 to 45) develop one of the loveliest titles for Mary in Latin devotion: *Mater misericordiae*, the "Mother of mercy". Hopkins finds a functional identification between Mary and mercy: We are "wound / With mercy round and round" just as we are by air, and that is because we are also so wound by the "wild web, wondrous robe" of Mary as it "Mantles the guilty globe". There are two implications. First, the mercy which is first and foremost an attribute of God, both in himself and in the saving economy whereby the Holy Trinity reaches out to us, is more palpably itself—that is, so far as human experience is concerned—when God wills that mercy to be mediated by Mary. Human beings respond more fully to the mercy of God when they receive it from the hands of a mother. Hopkins as believer experiences the Mother of the Lord not merely as an occasional dispenser of divine mercy but as that very mercy: "more than almoner, / The sweet alms' self

---

[109] Bernard of Clairvaux, *Sermo VII de Aquaeductu*.

is her". (Of course that must be understood in terms of the interrelation of finite and infinite discussed above.) The second implication can be stated more shortly, as Hopkins himself states it: "men are meant to share / Her life". It is an appeal to Christians who benefit from Mary's attention to make some effort consciously to reciprocate.

In lines 46 to 72 Hopkins restates the problem of a confession of the Blessed Virgin's universal mediation and develops, this time at more length, an explicitly Christological attempt to solve it. First, he reiterates the omnicompetence of Mary's gracious sub-mediation: "She holds high motherhood / Towards *all* our ghostly good" (emphasis added). It is her "part" to "lay"—allay, or lay low—concupiscence, man's potentially fatal trend, even after baptismal regeneration, toward evil, the "deathdance in his blood". This is the heart of what the ascetic tradition calls holy warfare, and nothing could be more pertinent to our final salvation. So, once again, how can a mere creature receive this role? Hopkins proposes an answer in terms of the mystery of Jesus Christ, the one and only (non-subordinated) "Mediator between God and men" (I Timothy 2:5). Any "part" Mary has consists, in one or another way, in disposing us to be the "place" where Jesus Christ comes to be in us. She has no part that will not be "Christ our Saviour still". He continues to take on—mysterically—substantial life in the faithful, as once he did *biologically* in the womb of her who is, in the words of ancient litany, the "Faith of all the faithful", the mother of all believers. Hopkins cries out with wonder—"O marvellous!"—at this truth of mystical theology, namely that Christ makes of his members "New Nazareths", "New Bethlems". And he finds here the key to the puzzle of Mary's universal task in our regard. Her role is precisely to "conceive / Him, morning, noon and eve" in us. And this explains how her mediation is both utterly comprehensive and yet altogether without derogation from the mediation of Christ. Hopkins emphasises that this is no abstruse theory, since it concerns the ultimate issue in practical reason: my personal raising to nobility of stature. What is at stake is "New self and nobler me". In his essay "On Personality, Grace and Freewill", Hopkins called the divine action in sanctifying a person and bringing him to the condition of deification "a lifting him from one self to another self, which is a most marvellous display of divine power".[110] God appropriately does this through Christ by way of Mary, since the unique Mediator is "Both God's and Mary's Son".

Hopkins would hardly be Hopkins if, thinking about air and its translucence, he did not look up at the sky. And so he bids the reader, "look overhead / How air is azurèd". On a fine day, the air above us is shot through with blue, "sapphire-shot", but that can hardly be said to "stain" light, to detract from its purity. Well, so it is with the grace of God when it comes to men through the hands of our blessed Lady. So far from distorting the real relations of God, man, and the redeemed creation, this Marian impregnation enables them to stand out with greater distinctness. "The glass-blue days are those / When every colour glows". And he adds that "this blue heaven / The seven or seven times seven / Hued sunbeam will transmit / Perfect, not alter it". Hopkins had worked out this aspect of the controlling analogy of the poem in a sermon given at Leigh in 1879:

> St Bernard's saying, All grace given through Mary: this is a mystery. Like blue sky, which for all its richness of colour does not stain the sunlight, though smoke and red clouds do, so God's graces come to us unchanged but all through

110 *Sermons*, 151.

her. Moreover she gladdens the Catholic's heaven and
when she is brightest so is the sun her Son.[111]

As Hopkins declares in the poetic version of this claim, if
some change in the light conditions on earth *does* have an
effect in terms of "Bloom breathe"—encouraging the opening of buds into blossom, then that "one breath more /
Earth is the fairer for".

Without that translucent yet protecting atmosphere, by
contrast, our earth would be unlivable, such as we can
assume planets of thin atmosphere too close to their own
suns to be. In an extraordinary disruption of tone, produc-
ing an infernal effect worthy of Milton (lines 94 to 102),
Hopkins imagines how, if air did not "slake" the sun's "fire",
the heavens would be transmogrified into a "grimy vasty
vault", the centre of the solar system a "blear and blinding
ball / With blackness bound". And lest we miss the point he
rubs it in. That is how men would look at deity were it not
for the Incarnation: "So God was god of old". The "limbs
like ours", which the humanised Word developed from the
body of the Virgin, are what endear the dreadful God of the
cosmic spaces to us. Were his glory—his majestic radiance—shown us "bare", either it would "blind" our minds
or at least "less would win" them. The interposing hand of
Mary, through which the glory shown in Christ is showered
down on us "leaves his light / Sifted to suit our sight".

The poem ends with a personal appeal from the poet to
the Mother of Christ to be with effect for him what he by
his words has declared her to be in principle for everyone.

---

[111] *Sermons*, 29.

Spelt from Sibyl's Leaves

EARNEST, earthless, equal, attuneable, ˈ vaulty, voluminous,
    . . . stupendous
Evening strains to be tíme's vást, ˈ womb-of-all, home-of-all,
    hearse-of-all night.
Her fond yellow hornlight wound to the west, ˈ her wild
    hollow hoarlight hung to the height
Waste; her earliest stars, earlstars, ˈ stárs principal, overbend
    us,
Fíre-féaturing heaven. For earth ˈ her being has unbound; her
    dapple is at end, as—
tray or aswarm, all throughther, in throngs; ˈ self ín self
steepèd and páshed—qúite
Disremembering, dísmémbering ˈ áll now. Heart, you round
    me right
With: Óur évening is over us; óur night ˈ whélms, whélms, ánd
    will end us.

Only the beakleaved boughs dragonish ˈ damask the tool-
    smooth bleak light; black,
Ever so black on it. Óur tale, O óur oracle ˈ Lét life, wáned, ah
    lét life wind
Off hér once skéined stained véined varíety ˈ upon, áll on twó
    spools; párt, pen, páck
Now her áll in twó flocks, twó folds—black, white; ˈ right,
    wrong; reckon but, reck but, mind
But thése two; wáre of a wórld where bút these ˈ twó tell, each
    off the óther; of a rack
Where, selfwrung, selfstrung, sheathe- and shelterless, ˈ thoúghts
    agaínst thoughts ín groans grínd.

. . . .

This poem was discovered in some notes later dubbed Hopkins's "Dublin Notebook" and so is generally dated to 1885 or thereafter. It is a strange, deeply sombre, thing, as befits its theme. It is also a technical marvel, transposing into English the effects of Welsh *cynghanedd* verse, and stretching the sonnet form to an extreme of its possibilities. What does it concern? The reader is justified in asking. And the answer is the end of the world, and with it final judgment: one of the *Novissima*, the "Last Things", which devout Catholics are expected to ponder, and which otherwise consist of death, hell, and heaven. But the eschatological scenario laid out here is not specifically Christian. The poem has a classical feel, and the reference in its title to the "Sibyl" is well chosen. Hopkins here takes on the mantle of the visionary prophetess who, in the Greco-Roman world, interpreted in cryptic terms the will of the gods for men on the basis, often enough, of natural portents. It is a feature of Catholic Christianity that it accepts the existence of elements of truth, goodness, and beauty in paganism. In the great fourteenth-century Latin hymn of doom and redemption, the *Dies irae*, the Sibyl appears testifying with David to the terror of the final dissolution of all things and the dread judgment of God on mortals. Hopkins will have been entirely familiar with that text since it formed part of the Mass of Requiem for the departed in the Roman Liturgy until 1969, and was set to great effect by such composers as Giuseppe Verdi (whose version could well be called, in Hopkins's word, "stupendous"). Verdi's French near-contemporary Gabriel Fauré refused to include it in his setting of the Requiem Mass on the grounds that it was far too minatory, despite the tender passages of appeal to the Redeemer that soften it. In 1969–70 the revisers of the Roman Missal demonstrated their agreement with Fauré, though the text subsequently reappeared in the Roman Liturgy of the Hours—the divine Office—subdivided as a set of hymns for the last week of the liturgical year. We can probably assume Hopkins would have taken the side of Verdi.

Hopkins's opening line, with seven seemingly ill-assorted but cumulatively ponderous adjectives, evokes, it would appear, the "last evening before Chaos takes total repossession of the universe".[112] This is the evening when God's final and irreversible judgment begins to take possession of the earth, palling the day in, first, dusk, and then darkness. Lastly, changes in the stellar world whereby the constellations start to "overbend" us disclose a "Fíre-féaturing heaven"— not altogether reassuring since in the context of the End of all things fire signifies not so much warmth and radiance as purgation and even destruction. The septet of introductory adjectives which set this scene are worth considering in their own right. This evening is "earnest"—owing to the gravity of what is purposed on it; it is "earthless"—in no way depending on biological or human processes; "equal"—impartial in the way it operates; "attuneable"—inexorably consistent in what it signifies; "vaulty" and "voluminous"—immense in the scale of what is projected. Hopkins, who had studied Vergil's *Aeneid* both at Highgate School and at Oxford may have had in mind the passage soon after the opening of Book Six where the Sibyl introduces Aeneas to the underworld in search of his father who is to give him a revelation. In lines 270–72 of the epic, Virgil describes their journey as taking place in a "gloom when things can still be seen but lose their colour".[113] This neatly captures the atmosphere of

[112] N. H. MacKenzie, *A Reader's Guide to Gerard Manley Hopkins*, 160.

[113] K. Quinn, *Virgil's "Aeneid". A Critical Description* (London 1968), 165.

Hopkins's own poem, from which the medley of variegated
light-suffused tones that dominate in his descriptive verse has
been stripped away. All takes place, as Virgil would put it,
sola sub nocte, "exclusively in the gloom of night", the night
that Hopkins calls "womb-of-all, home-of-all, hearse-of-all",
because it now covers birth, life, and death indifferently.
And so despite the persistence in the sky of remote after-
effects of sunset—whether the usual after-glow ("hornlight")
or the less common astronomical feature called "zodiacal
light" ("hoarlight"), "earth ᅵ her being has unbound; her /
dapple is at end". Hopkins could not imagine a world
deprived, through this Stygean gloom, of "dapple"—the
quintessence of pied beauty. Its loss is therefore the unbind-
ing of earth's being, it is ontological collapse. The "fond yellow" and "wild hollow" of the disappearing light are
Hopkins's tribute to the old heavens and the old earth which
vanish in creation's fearful remaking. The ruptured speech
that articulates this collapse: "as— / tray or aswarm, all
throughther, in throngs; ᅵ self ín self / steepèd and páshed—
qúite", conveys by its stammering eloquence the disintegration of scapes into formlessness. Both psychic nature and
physical nature are dissolving, there is "disremembering" as
well as "dísmémbering". The vision makes the heart warn
("round") the poet: Death, which is the End of all things *for
me*, and so a microcosmic version of the macrocosmic scene
he envisages, will come to him as to Everyman. "Óur évening is over us; óur night ᅵ whélms, whélms, ánd will end us."
Thus the octet of the sonnet closes.

    If we expect the sestet to give us a quite different story we
shall be disappointed. Hopkins confirms the tone of the
octet before going on to draw the moral. In an ending world
drained of colour with the light, the trees, once such a
delight to the poet, show only bare and in context sinister
outlines: "beakleaved boughs dragonish", laying patterns

("damask") on the "tool-smoothed bleak light". Nature is now so comfortless as almost to appear its own antithesis: armed and metallic, like Viking ships with their dragon-prows or damascened swords. But this unrelieved outer blackness brings home the moral truth of our lives. No matter how chromatically varied they have been in dramatic or picturesque detail, enjoyable material for autobiography, the "once skéined stained véined varíety", they must revolve themselves into primary black and white. For all his Paterian love of living intensely through aesthetic experiences of God in the cosmos, Hopkins declares in the sestet that, actually, we shall be judged on our good or evil deeds. The judgment of our past and present, and so our destiny in the future, will be wound on the "two spools" of right and wrong. As in the Gospel parable of the Grand Assize (Matthew 25:31–46), the crucial discrimination will be between those who performed works of mercy to the anonymous Lord hidden in their fellow humans and those who did no such things. This will be the parting, each into its own "pen, páck". The "twó flocks, twó folds" of the sheep and goats are what above all in life we should "reckon" with, or "mind". Hopkins could now, if he wished, lighten our darkness by an evocation of the reward of the righteous. But he prefers to leave us with his own inimitable evocation of Hell, which he depicts as an endless gyration of the self in its own obsessive thoughts. In his sermons, Hopkins developed a philosophical theology for the life of the separated soul.

> After death the soul is left to its own resources, with only the scapes and *species* of its past life; which being unsupplemented or undisplaced by a fresh continual current of experience, absorb and press upon its consciousness.[114]

---

[114] *Sermons*, 139.

For the blessed, this pressure is—well—blessedness. For the damned it turns to the torment Hopkins describes in the last words of this poem: where "selfwrung, selfstrung, sheathe- and shelterless, ǀ thóughts / agaínst thoughts ín groans grínd".

To what serves Mortal Beauty?

TO what serves mortal beauty ǀ —dangerous; does set danc-
ing blood—the O-seal-that-so ǀ feature, flung prouder form
Than Purcell tune lets tread to? ǀ See: it does this: keeps warm
Men's wits to the things that are; ǀ what good means—where
      a glance
Master more may than gaze, ǀ gaze out of countenance.
Those lovely lads once, wet-fresh ǀ windfalls of war's storm,
How then should Gregory, a father, ǀ have gleanèd else from
      swarm-
èd Rome? But God to a nation ǀ dealt that day's dear chance.
To man, that needs would worship ǀ block or barren stone,
Our law says: Love what are ǀ love's worthiest, were all known;
World's loveliest—men's selves. Self ǀ flashes off frame and
      face.
What do then? how meet beauty? ǀ Merely meet it; own,
Home at heart, heaven's sweet gift; ǀ then leave, let that alone.
Yea, wish that though, wish all, ǀ God's better beauty, grace.

·   ·   ·   ·   ·   ·   ·

This poem was written on 23 August 1885, while Hopkins
was on Retreat at Clongowes College in County Kildare. It
tries to answer the question raised by "Spelt from Sibyl's
Leaves" in the light of the joyous exultation in nature and
the God of nature found in, for instance, the sonnets of the
St Beuno's period, and indeed the delight in the human
form which entered into his emotional response to those in
his pastoral care, according to the "priestly" poems of the

Oxford and Liverpool years. "To what serves Mortal Beauty" was an almost inescapable subject of reflection in these juxtaposed circumstances.

Hopkins's first thought is of the *danger* to the soul which mortal beauty represents. Everyday experience proves it can raise demons: notably the demon of lust in those who are attracted by it, since it "does set danc- / ing blood", and the demon of pride in those who are the possessors of it, if one happens to have an "O-seal-that-so-feature" kind of face—the sort of face, in other words, artists would long to perpetuate. Such beauty readily becomes a "flung prouder form", an exhibitionist vaunting of one's looks, and the poet contrasts this with the measured self-assertion of the music of his favourite composer, Henry Purcell. So far, so bad. But this is not the whole story. Beauty also has a positive role in human experience: it "keeps warm / Men's wits to the things that are". In other words, beauty has the desirable effect of disturbing the lazy observer, the somnolent soul, the casually self-preoccupied idling mind. Beauty wakes us up to give what Newman called "real" rather than "notional" assent to realities other than ourselves. (As a young man, Hopkins had wanted to produce a popular version of the *Essay in Aid of a Grammar of Assent* where Newman lays out that idea, but Newman did not consider his book needed *haute-vulgarisation*.) Hopkins stresses the role of intelligence in this—"men's wits", and the affective tone he has in mind is warmth—"keep warm / Men's wits". Beauty, then, kindles the mind to love. Writing to Robert Bridges, Hopkins arranged orders of beauty hierarchically. Physical beauty comes lowest, though "no one can admire beauty of the body more than I do"; next comes such mental beauty as is found in genius; but the highest kind of beauty, he wrote, is beauty of character: the "handsome heart".[115] We can surely hear at this point Jowett's pupil recalling the lessons of Plato's *Symposium*—but doing so through the lens of the special concern of the English moralists of the eighteenth and nineteenth century with *moral character.*

Just because beauty is even in its lowest form a stimulant and stirrer, shaking us out of routine living and catalysing new trains of thought, it "Master more may than gaze". Beauty can effect more than simply the gratified glance. And Hopkins's chief piece of evidence for this claim is a favourite story from the English Catholic heritage. As recounted in the Venerable Bede's *History of the English Church and People*, it was the beauty of face and form of some Anglo-Saxon prisoners of war in the Roman slave-market—in Hopkins's words, "Those lovely lads once, wet-fresh │ windfalls of war's storms" that led the bishop of Rome, Pope Gregory I, as he was passing, to ask after their country of origin, whereupon he produced the first of two atrocious Latin puns, calling them "not Angles so much as angels".[116] Thus began in St Gregory's mind the process of deliberation which issued eventually in the decision to send the Roman monk Augustine, with his companions, to initiate the conversion of Kent and eventually all England south of the Humber. Hopkins points out that historians know of no other proximate cause for this apostolic venture by the Roman see. "How then should Gregory, a father │ have gleanèd else from swarm- / èd Rome?" By calling Rome "swarm- / èd' Hopkins implies that so tumultuously populous a city, of which Gregory, *faute de mieux*, was civil as well as ecclesiastical ruler, could never have led him to focus on this far-off island of which men knew little or nothing if

[115] *Letters,* 95.
[116] St Bede the Venerable, *Historia ecclesiastica gentis Anglorum,* II. 1.

beauty had not arrested his attention and, in due course, lent ardour to his mind. Hopkins find this conclusive evidence for the way divine Providence uses even beauty of body: "God to a nation I dealt that day's dear chance".

The heathen in his blindness bows down to wood and stone, and so did the Germanic pagan ancestors of the Christian English. At the opening of the sestet Hopkins notes the fact and contrasts it with "our law"—the Christian code which replaced that of the Teutonic tribal system in the course of the Anglo-Saxon period. "Our law" calls on us to love what is most worthy of love, and that is the loveliest thing in the world—"men's selves". By adding in parenthesis "were all known" Hopkins hints at the theological mystery involved here. The foundation of Christian anthropology is the revealed doctrine, attested in the Book of Genesis, that man was created "in the image of God, to his likeness"—and the New Testament letters will confirm this, giving it moreover a Christological climax and rationale. The *reason* why human beings are "world's loveliest" is a reason furnished only by revelation. They are living icons of the unseen God, adumbrations of the perfect image which is Jesus Christ.

But then the further question arises, how do we engage with men's "selves", how do we come to know them, enjoy communion with them? Hopkins's answer is "Self I flashes off frame and face". We might think of Ludwig Wittgenstein's dictum that the body is the best picture of the soul. Hopkins will not be satisfied, however, until he has turned all this into a programme for action and reaction. With such a programme he leaves us. It proves to consist in two maxims. The first is that, when we recognise beauty of "frame and face" we should be content gratefully to acknowledge it as a gift from the Creator—"Merely meet it; own . . . heaven's sweet gift". The emphasis here is on the "merely" as the practical corollary that follows makes plain: "then leave, let that alone". And the second maxim is that we should wish its bearer "God's better beauty, grace", since only this enables the image of God in man to shine forth as was intended by its divine Author, who is also all beauty's archetypal Source.

The Terrible Sonnets

WHILE ALL the critics agree such sonnets certainly exist, there is no full consensus on their number. Here they are treated as six in all. If chronological exactitude is sought, the sequence in which these six should be arranged is unknown. I follow the conjectural reconstruction by Robert Bernard Martin, who writes:

> Although we have no proof of the actual sequence in which he composed the Terrible Sonnets, they can easily be put in a rough progression that seems to parallel his emotions in 1885 as we guess them from other sources, so that they have some of the effect of a sonnet sequence, even if that was probably far from Hopkins's purpose.[117]

The name "Terrible Sonnets", incidentally, is owed to Robert Bridges. Norman MacKenzie, with uncharacteristic levity, calls it a "rather risky title".[118] Other possibilities are "the Sonnets of Desolation" (W. H. Gardner's proposal), or "the Dark Sonnets" (MacKenzie's own). Their nature may best be introduced by citing Hopkins's letter to Bridges in May 1885 where he says of one of them (just which is unclear), it was "written in blood".[119]

---

[117] R. B. Martin, *Gerard Manley Hopkins*, 385.
[118] N. H. MacKenzie, *A Reader's Guide to Gerard Manley Hopkins*, 171.
[119] *Letters*, 219.

1.

To seem the stranger

TO seem the stranger lies my lot, my life
Among strangers. Father and mother dear,
Brothers and sisters are in Christ not near
And he my peace / my parting, sword and strife.

England, whose honour O all my heart woos, wife
To my creating thought, would neither hear
Me, were I pleading, plead nor do I: I wear-
y of idle a being but by where wars are rife.

I am in Ireland now; now I am at a third
Remove. Not but in all removes I can
Kind love both give and get. Only what word

Wisest my heart breeds dark heaven's baffling ban
Bars or hell's spell thwarts. This to hoard unheard,
Heard unheeded, leaves me a lonely began.

. . . .

The case for placing this sonnet first is simply that in it
Hopkins lays out what he can of the rational grounds for his
unhappiness. Their inadequacy for settling his mind under-
lies the remaining five. "To seem the stranger" gives voice to
Hopkins's deep sense of loneliness, estrangement, frustra-
tion in his various interlocked vocations as Catholic, priest,
scholar, and poet. His conversion from Anglicanism to
Rome brought about his original alienation from loved
ones—though after the initial shock to his family the extent
to which Hopkins magnified this problem beyond its real
boundaries is a moot point. At any rate in his perception
there was now a deep divide. He saw his own case as—not

of course unusually in Victorian England—fulfilling the predictions of Jesus in St Matthew's Gospel: "[A] man's foes will be those of his own household" (10:36). As recorded by Matthew, while announcing his message would separate kinsmen like a sword (v. 34), the Saviour had conceded that, at one level, he would diminish peace, not augment it. But Hopkins was aware of other texts, supremely in St John's Gospel, where Christ promised at a deeper level to leave his own peace with the disciples (14:27), the peace that was his typical post-Easter greeting to them (20:19; 21:26), so much so that the entire Gospel could be summed up by St Paul as "the gospel of peace" (Ephesians 6:15). Painfully, Hopkins had verified both the negative and the positive together, and the hard-to-bear paradox that they had the same source—"he my peace / my parting, sword and strife". The next hurtful rift was with "England". Hopkins's English patriotism—probably more than British, despite his Welsh connexions—was heartfelt and profound. Here he maintains that only through coupling with England can his mind be fertile ("England, . . . wife to my creating thought"). Perhaps by way of the English language and the Oxonian cast of his intellectual formation this was true. How had England made clear she would spurn him: "England, . . . would neither hear / Me, were I pleading, plead nor do I"? Possibly through the rejection by the most sympathetic English cultural organ he was likely to encounter, the Jesuit-owned *Month*, of the two "shipwreck poems" he had submitted there, one of which, "The Wreck of the Deutschland", is his greatest work, and both of which end with a plea for the reconversion of England to the Catholic faith. Now he no longer sought to have such pleas brought into the public forum. As a consequence, so far as the conversion of England was concerned, he stood idle, a mere bystander "where wars are rife", and this in itself made him "weary" in soul.

Presumably he could scarcely have called himself idle when he was engaged on the "English mission", as the Catholic religious orders and congregations in exile in France and the Low Countries called their pastoral and apostolic works in the home country. So there is a natural transition to its third grievance, which is his Irish exile, which put him at a "third / Remove" from his heart's desires. Conscious, maybe, that not just once or twice he had been offered generous hospitality by Irish people (all Catholic Unionists, it can be noted) and in one case the friendship of a Jesuit of the Irish Province, Hopkins accepts that, even in Ireland, "I can / Kind love both give and get". But why were all his efforts to be productive, creative, generative—whether academically, or poetically or in terms of more strictly priestly endeavours—so ill-starred? If there is not something Satanic about the way he is dogged (in which case, "hell's spell thwarts"), then he is left to draw an even more frightening inference. The God of grace and salvation seemed to have withdrawn from Hopkins's life, to be replaced by a surrogate Deity whose ways are either maleficent or arbitrary: "dark heaven's baffling ban". All the treasures Hopkins has accumulated from experience, study, reflection are thus useless, and himself a "lonely began", left behind by life, not excluding—indeed very much including—spiritual life.

2.

I wake and feel

I WAKE and feel the fell of dark, not day.
What hours, O what black hoürs we have spent
This night! what sights you, heart, saw; ways you went!
And more must, in yet longer light's delay.

With witness I speak this. But where I say
Hours I mean years, mean life. And my lament
Is cries countless, cries like dead letters sent
To dearest him that lives alas! away.

I am gall, I am heartburn. God's most deep decree
Bitter would have me taste: my taste was me;
Bones built in me, flesh filled, blood brimmed the curse.

Selfyeast of spirit a dull dough sours. I see
The lost are like this, and their scourge to be
As I am mine, their sweating selves; but worse.

    .   .   .   .

"To seem the stranger" ends with an overwrought conclusion. A rosier construction could be placed on most if not all the negative facets of his biography Hopkins had passed in review. Almost inevitably, Hopkins would ask himself whether he had not become his own worst enemy. In "I wake and feel" he recognises the self-tormenting from which he seems unable to escape.

The sonnet opens with a horrible image. Hopkins awakes and senses not the daylight from the open heavens he so loved but a darkness, which, in his present state, feels like the hairy hide—the "fell"—of some predatory beast: As an adjective "fell" indicates malevolence, and as a noun it bears the additional sense of a—presumably desolate and trackless—moorland waste. At about this time, Hopkins registered, in his letters and private meditations, his fear that he was entering madness. He laments the "black hours" he has spent sleepless in the past night, tortured by irrepressible mental images, and recurring destructive thoughts, and fears more of the same thing unless daybreak comes quickly. In his over-taxed condition he generalises from those hours to years and indeed his entire life: "where I say / Hours I mean years, mean life". His "cries countless" appear to have no corresponding recipient. The gracious God having hidden his face from Hopkins, all his prayers are "like dead letters sent / To dearest him that lives alas! away". We note the "dearest him". In all his trials, Hopkins never seems to have encountered temptations against faith or love—though he certainly knew temptations against the remaining member of the trio of theological virtues, hope. In some private meditation notes of roughly this time he speaks of entering on "that course of loathing and hopelessness which I have so often felt before".[120]

It is already amazing that such personal anguish, whereby the subject feels himself losing control of his emotions, could be poured into so restrained and exact a vehicle as the sonnet form. The "turn" of the poem is hardly going to reveal a cheerful Hopkins casting off the mask. What happens in the sestet is, rather, a change of imagery which now becomes prevailingly medical in character. Hopkins, who was not in good physical shape at this time, whether for reasons psychosomatic or otherwise, compares himself to a victim of severe jaundice whose bile courses through his whole system even to the point of discolouring his skin tissue and the whites of his eyes: "I am gall." Owing to its taste when it reaches the mouth, the bile, thus pathologically discharged, tastes bitter. Hopkins finds bitter the special providence that, he considers, has thus brought him low. "God's most deep decree / Bitter would have me taste". And no single aspect of his being is unaffected: "my taste was me". In the year before his death he wrote in some retreat notes that the mind cannot "be at rest as long as something bitter distils in it and it aches".[121] Prophetically,

---

[120] *Sermons,* 261–62.
[121] Ibid., 262.

Hopkins had recorded in advance the absolute pervasiveness through the self that such a "distillation" can attain.

> [A]bove all my shame, my guilt, my fate are the very things in feeling, in tasting, which I must taste that self-taste which nothing in the world can match.[122]

And soon the medical turns to the infernal: "blood brimmed the curse". The spirit should by rights make one's whole being rise, but the "yeast" Hopkins generates only has the effect of turning sour the unresponsive "dough" of his mind and body. And what is this if not hellish? "I see / The lost are like this". The real punishment of the damned is to be who they are: "their scourge to be . . . their sweating selves". As he put it in his sermons: "[N]o worm but themselves gnaws them and gnaws no one but themselves". And, says Hopkins, I resemble them. It has been conjectured that, by adding "but worse", especially in an early draft where these words sit closer to the self-reference "As I am mine", Hopkins at some point considered his condition more lamentable than that of those in hell. Not only doctrinal orthodoxy, for which he was a stickler, but common sense too should rule this interpretation out. As the next sonnet shows, things were bad enough.

3.
No worst, there is none

NO worst, there is none. Pitched past pitch of grief,
More pangs will, schooled at forepangs, wilder wring.
Comforter, where, where is your comforting?
Mary, mother of us, where is your relief?

122 Ibid., 125.

My cries heave, herds-long; huddle in a main, a chief-
woe, world-sorrow; on an age-old anvil wince and sing—
Then lull, then leave off. Fury had shrieked 'No ling-
ering! Let me be fell: force I must be brief'.
O the mind, mind has mountains; cliffs of fall
Frightful, sheer, no-man-fathomed. Hold them cheap
May who ne'er hung there. Nor does long our small
Durance deal with that steep or deep. Here! creep,
Wretch, under a comfort serves in a whirlwind: all
Life death does end and each day dies with sleep.

. . . .

This sonnet represents the nadir of Hopkins's interior suffering. The opening words probably pick up Edgar of Glouces-
ter's tortured monologue in Act IV, scene 1, of Shakespeare's
The Tragedy of King Lear, and English literature hardly knows
a more gut-wrenching moment. "Pitched past pitch of
grief", on the other hand, is pure Hopkins. That is owing to
the technical force attached to the word "pitch" in a vocabulary for the ontology of selfhood he had worked out in
kinder days. This term for the energetic instress of all duly
selved being is now crossed, however, by other currents of
meaning—as when someone is "pitched", caught off balance
and hurled against their will, and may be so thrust—who
knows?—into pitch darkness. That benighted atmosphere,
after all, would be cognate with "I wake and feel".

The cumulative character of negative experience which,
by inducing brooding and depression, makes us ever more
ill-prepared for its renewed onset—we become "schooled at
forepangs"—leads Hopkins to seek some recourse beyond
the self. In the Gospel of St John Jesus reveals that one of
names of the Holy Spirit is *Parakleitos*, perhaps best trans-
lated "Advocate", since the primary context is legal, but the

rendering "Comforter" has entered English via the Latin *Consolator* of Jerome and Augustine. The traditional imagery of Catholicism points in many ways to a special relationship between the economies of the Holy Spirit and the Mother of God, and one linguistic sign of this is Mary's title *consolatrix*, which occurs in the best-known Marian Litany, the *Lauretana* or Litany of Loreto, in the form "consoler of the afflicted".[123] Hopkins brackets these two together, calling first on the third divine Person and then on the Mother of the Lord, but he finds, to no avail. No "comforting", no "relief", is forthcoming.

That Hopkins is by now utterly self-obsessed and numbed to the sufferings of others is belied by the image, strange as it is, that follows. His lament is only that of one creature, but entire herds of suffering human animals "huddle". He knows full well his pain belongs with a greater *Weltschmerz*, a "world-sorrow". What is especially hard to bear is the reiterative character of sufferings that seem to pass only to recur, perhaps intensified, like hammer-blows on an anvil.

The sestet tells of the upshot. Hopkins compares the agony of the mind that can find no ease to the situation of a mountaineer clinging to a rock-face above a precipice so deep it is an abyss. The mind *has* such "mountains" and only those who have never "hung there" would depreciate the terror they involve. If this "steep or deep" becomes a chronic experience, no one can "hang in there" long. Ours is "small durance". The best hope Hopkins holds out is to find some overhanging ledge that may give temporary shelter as in a whirlwind. He bids those like him (but chiefly himself): "creep, / Wretch". As the sonnet seems to borrow its opening

[123] A. Nichols, OP, *Come to the Father. An Invitation to Share the Catholic Faith* (London 2000), 65–66.

words from *King Lear*, so there may be an allusion here to
the ruined Lear's taking refuge in a "hovel" in Act III, scene
2, of the play. But Hopkins's real "hope" is for death, which
has the unique merit of bringing life to its close.

4.

Carrion Comfort

NOT, I'll not, carrion comfort, Despair, not feast on thee;
Not untwist—slack they may be—these last strands of man
In me ór, most weary, cry *I can no more*. I can;
Can something, hope, wish day come, not choose not to be.

But ah, but O thou terrible, why wouldst thou rude on me
Thy wring-world right foot rock? lay a lionlimb against me?
    scan
With darksome devouring eyes my bruisèd bones? and fan,
O in turns of tempest, me heaped there; me frantic to avoid
    thee and flee?

Why? That my chaff might fly; my grain lie, sheer and clear.
Nay in all that toil, that coil, since (seems) I kissed the rod,
Hand rather, my heart lo! lapped strength, stole joy, would
    laugh, chéer.
Cheer whom though? The hero whose heaven-handling flung
    me, fóot tród
Me? or me that fought him? O which one? is it each one?
    That night, that year
Of now done darkness I wretch lay wrestling with (my God!)
    my God.

· · · · · · ·

We naturally ask ourselves, At this juncture was Hopkins
suicidal? "Carrion Comfort" would seem to deal with such

a temptation, naming it and eventually shaming it for what it is. As Martin puts it, he "seems both to touch bottom and to begin swimming upward once more".[124] The title, or opening words of the sonnet, once heard, is never forgotten. Despair is "carrion comfort" because, in its own dreadful way, as final yielding to hopelessness, it is comfort of a sort. Like vultures picking at a carcase it is feeding on (spiritual) death. But Hopkins declares, "I'll not . . . feast on thee". Even though Hopkins feels himself holding onto his humanity only by a few "last strands of man" he is not going to "untwist" them. He will not cry, as he might, "I can no more". Reduced to an extremity as he is, he is at least capable of something. He can "not choose not to be". A tiny flicker of self-affirmation, though feeble, still exists.

In the second quatrain of the octet a rush of self-defensive anger shows it can burst into flame. The identity of Hopkins's enemy—"O thou terrible"—has been much discussed. Is it Despair, or is it God? The ambiguity is surely deliberate. The Book of Job, where the protagonist's impassioned speeches bear a resemblance to this poem, has a "Satan" who is at once the destructive tempter of man and the lawful instrument of the God who would test his servants to find of what mettle they are made. (To say as much is the point of Job's prologue and epilogue.) In the context of the two quatrains, the reader's natural assumption is that personified despair remains the poem's other agent. And the monstrous diction would seem to bear this out. Hopkins's foe tramples him with his "wring-world right foot", that is as fell as weapon as a flung rock or a (presumably clawed) "lionlimb". This surreal figure "scans" him with "darksome devouring eyes" like a chief of the Orcs in J. R. R. Tolkien's *The Lord of the Rings*. And as if his enemy has

---

[124] R. B. Martin, *Gerard Manley Hopkins,* 386.

magical powers to summon the world's elements against
him, Hopkins feels himself—"me heaped there"—blasted
by the storms his tormentor brings down on his prostrate
form. No wonder he is "frantic" to "flee".

But the turn of the sonnet raises a doubt in our minds.
The verb Hopkins had used for this spiritual-meteorological
assault was to "fan", and when as the sestet opens he puts the
question "Why?", the answer that comes has all the hallmarks
of the biblical divine Judge standing ready for action at his
threshing-floor. "Why? That my chaff might fly; my grain lie,
sheer and clear". John the Baptist warned his hearers of the
judgment to come from the imminently expected Messiah:

> His winnowing fork is in his hand, to clear his threshing-
> floor and to gather the wheat into his granary, but the chaff
> he will burn with unquenchable fire (Luke 3:17).

Hopkins had written a meditation on this very text where
he describes the fan as a kind of scoop in which grain is
tossed with violence against the wind, thus bringing about
a highly visible separation of chaff blown away and grain
lying "heaped" on one side.[125]

In the hard labour, "toil", and constraining complexities,
"coil", of his life since he "kissed the rod" of obedience to
the divine will through entering on the Jesuit priesthood
with all its hardships for him, something supremely positive
has been under way. He can even write that his hand and his
heart "lapped strength", a phrase intensified in the succeeding formulae "stole joy" and "would laugh, chéer". Some
secret spiritual joy, possibly connected with the drinking of
the Eucharistic chalice, the cup of gladness, gives cheer.

The final tercet enquires, pertinently, "Cheer whom
though?" Clarifying the point leads us (as it led Hopkins)

---

[125] *Sermons*, 267–68.

to two discoveries. First, the seeming "enemy" of the octet
was God in Christ after all, the "hero whose heaven-handling flung / me, fóot tród / Me". Secondly, was the "joy"
really Hopkins', or was it not rather Christ's? Or perhaps,
was it for and from both of them together? In the year of
darkness (1884–85), Hopkins, like Jacob at the Ford of the
Jabbok, had been wrestling with the Lord. In the Genesis
story (32:22–32), Jacob is hurt and yet in a sense wins the
contest, since he will not let the mysterious Stranger go
until the latter has blessed him. Hence Hopkins's whispered
conclusion: "Of now done darkness I wretch lay wrestling
with (my God!) / my God".

5.

Patience

PATIENCE, hard thing! the hard thing but to pray,
But bid for, Patience is! Patience who asks
Wants war, wants wounds; weary his times, his tasks;
To do without, take tosses, and obey.

Rare patience roots in these, and, these away,
Nowhere. Natural heart's ivy Patience masks
Our ruins of wrecked past purpose. There she basks
Purple eyes and seas of liquid leaves all day.

We hear our hearts grate on themselves: it kills
To bruise them dearer. Yet the rebellious wills
Of us we do bid God bend to him even so.

And where is he who more and more distils
Delicious kindness?—He is patient. Patience fills
His crisp combs, and that comes those ways we know.

· · · · · · ·

In "Patience" Hopkins, his worst grief assuaged, asks for strength and endurance. The virtue of patience, lauded by St Ignatius in his *Rules for the Discernment of Spirits*, is somewhat ambivalent. It makes no sense to seek to develop it unless one is fairly sure of an ongoing life of affliction. That is why Hopkins finds it a "hard thing", hard even to "pray" or "bid" for. Patience "wants"—calls out for—"war" and "wounds". And, reflects Hopkins ruefully, he has certainly known them in the past. Not only has there been the (not by any means always inspiring) grind of the religious life: "weary his times, his tasks". He has also taken "tosses", since so many of the things he was asked to do as Jesuit somehow failed to reach proper fruition. And yet he obeyed. These conflicts are the sign that, truly, this has been a war of virtues against vices. "Rare patience roots in these, and, these away, / Nowhere." Here Hopkins introduces the botanical imagery which will dominate the rest of the octet. "Patience" also named a plant—one of the knotweeds, a relative of sorrel. *Rumex patientia* was, as Hopkins says, relatively rare. A European import, it was chiefly known as a pot-herb, but it occasionally became naturalised on, significantly, "a few waste and grassy places".[126] Perhaps because the botanical patience was not exactly a household word, Hopkins subtly shifts the focus to another and better known plant. Patience (the virtue) is "Natural heart's-ivy". As Donald McChesney remarks, this is "a satisfying image of a slow, soft, concealing growth spreading over cracks and barrenness".[127] In days before a more invasive curatorial system for ancient monuments was invented, the ruined masonry Victorian Englishmen saw was likely to be ivy-covered. And this Hopkins hopes—and even reports—is the patience-wrapped condition of his own heart.

It is a bittersweet comparison. In the eighteenth century,

[126] R. Mabey, *Flora Britannica,* 111.
[127] D. McChesney, *A Hopkins Commentary,* 162.

admirers of the picturesque took ivy as a symbol of melancholy. But in the succeeding century, drawing to its close as Hopkins was writing, ivy was considered beautiful and even festal in character.[128] Concealing the "ruins of wrecked past purpose" sounds a sad occupation. But what follows is lyrical: the dark berries of the ivy are like "purple eyes", belonging to creatures that "bask . . . all day" on "seas of liquid leaves". The virtue, once acquired, or, if given supernaturally, infused, transforms the sharp, uncomfortable edges of a seemingly ruined life into something soft and almost soporific. That may not sound Ignatian. But in fact, in the *Rules for the Discernment of Spirits*—the most patristic element in Loyola's spirituality, reaching far back to the fifth century Greek monk Diadochus of Photike—patience makes of experiences of "desolation" a preamble to their opposite, *consolation*.

The sestet, however, seems far in mood from so desirable an outcome. The sound Hopkins's heart makes is not soothing but *grating*. He fears that to take more bruising would *kill* off the heart's affections altogether. His response to these warning signs and anxieties is ruthless. The poet will ask God to "bend" the more his rebellious will—until it comes close to breaking is how some commentators, and among them the Jesuit editor of Hopkins's *Sermons and Devotional Writings*, have completed the thought.[129] It is not especially Catholic to make duty and obligation the driving force of moral action. "Moralism" overtaxes nature by insinuating arbitrariness or mechanical imposition from without.[130] On the other hand, who can deny there are situations where only sheer dogged fidelity to our engagements sees us through.

---

[128] R. Mabey, *Flora Brittanica*, 276–82.

[129] *Sermons*, 218.

[130] See for an antidote D. Schindler, "Is Truth Ugly? Moralism and the Convertibility of Being and Love", *Communio* 27 (2000): 701–28.

That Hopkins was not a closet Jansenist who found the be-all and end-all of morals and spirituality in pleasing and appeasing a demanding God is made plain in the sonnet's last tercet. Would a temperamental Jansenist name God the Distiller of "Delicious kindness"? Syrup, or some sweet liqueur, is Hopkins's word-association here for grace.

God's patience, reflects Hopkins, is indefinitely more remarkable than our own. Salvation history attests to it on the macrocosmic level, when dealing with our race—and microcosmically, when treating individuals, in the lives of the saints. His "combs" are filled with the stuff: Here Hopkins is thinking, surely, of Psalm 118, the psalm in praise of the Torah (which means God's Law, yes, but also God's *teaching*). For the Psalmist, the words of the Torah are "sweeter than honey, honey from the comb" (v. 103). And so the "syrup" was revelation's honey, the "sweet liqueur", its mead. That gives us the key for understanding the poem's last five words, "that comes those ways we know". Not, then, the way Hopkins knows from consulting individual experience. His notebooks and letters of the period prove otherwise. But the "ways we know": we Catholic Christians take our bearings in these matters not solipsistically, from our autobiographies, but from the entire public record of God's gracious dealings with mankind.

6.

My own heart

MY own heart let me have more pity on; let
Me live to my sad self hereafter kind,
Charitable; not live this tormented mind
With this tormented mind tormenting yet.

I cast for comfort I can no more get
By groping round my comfortless, than blind
Eyes in their dark can day or thirst can find
Thirst's all-in-all in all a world of wet.

Soul, self; come, poor Jackself, I do advise
You, jaded, let be; call off thoughts awhile
Elsewhere; leave comfort root-room; let joy size

As God knows when to God knows what; whose smile
's not wrung, see you; unforeseen times rather—as skies
Betweenpie mountains—lights a lovely mile.

·   ·   ·   ·   ·   ·   ·

In this poem Hopkins's wisdom in his own regard reasserts
itself. Perhaps it might be less inadequate to say that he
allows the love of God for him to be, since all three key
terms of this change of heart—pity, kindness, charity—are
ascribed first and foremost in the biblical tradition to God
himself. As he had known better as an undergraduate than
later, there is not only a natural but also a Christian love of
self which has nothing to do with selfishness.[131] What use
can we be to others if we are constantly mired in self-
hatred? As St Thomas puts it with his customary clarity and
frankness, our love for ourselves is *forma et radix amicitiae*,
"the model and root of friendship", since "our friendship
for others consists precisely in the fact that our attitude to
them is the same as to ourselves".[132] This is as biblical (cf.
Leviticus 19:18, Thomas's starting point in this article of
the *Summa theologiae*) as it is Hellenic. And just this combination of impetus from revelation with the recovery of
natural sanity was needed if Hopkins were to break out

---

131 *Journals*, 124.
132 *Summa theologiae* IIa. IIae., q. 25, a. 4, corpus.

from the cycle of self-accusation which the sonnet's opening quatrain captures in its repeated use of words formed
from that infernal word "torment".

So Hopkins begins to search, somewhat feverishly, for
"comfort": "I cast for comfort . . . / By groping round my
comfortless". There is something alarming about the way the
final adjective qualifies no noun, as though in his disorienta-
tion Hopkins cannot put a name to the human "space" he is
occupying. All he knows is, by dint of thinking he can no
more summon up the comfort he needs than a blind man
can require the light of day to enter his eyes or a shipwrecked
sailor wracked with thirst render potable the saline waters
around him. It has been pointed out that, actually, Hopkins's
comparison is not for his own neediness to a thirsty man, but
to *thirst itself*. It is "thirst" that cannot "find / Thirst's all-in-
all in all a world of wet", and this adds peculiar vividness to
the image.[133] There are echoes here of Samuel Taylor
Coleridge's *The Rhyme of the Ancient Mariner*. The Mariner,
notoriously, had to show a touch of pity to himself before
the saints could bestow pity on him.

In the sestet, perhaps encouraged by memories of
Coleridge's poem (there is no reason why literature should
not be a vehicle for grace), Hopkins renews the capacity to
give himself good counsel with which the sonnet began. He
addresses himself—"Soul, self; . . . poor Jackself"—with a
curious combination of detachment and affection which,
psychologically, is a good start. (A "Jack" was a common term
for a sailor so possibly the Mariner is still the example in his
mind's eye, though no doubt the primary denotation is Hopkins as overworked academic drudge.) The medicine he now
applies to himself—"leave comfort root-room; let joy size /
As God knows when to God know what"—would have been

---

133 R. Boyle, SJ, *Metaphor in Hopkins* (Chapel Hill, NC 1961), 147.

well understood by such medieval mystics as Meister Eck-hart, who coined for it the term *Gelassenheit.* "Letting-be", "letting-go", "self-abandonment": all this means, in the context of the Christian ascetical and mystical tradition, letting God be God. God's favours cannot be "wrung" out of him. They come nevertheless, and probably when one is least expecting it. Hopkins ends with a radiant image that brings together his old joy in the natural creation and a refound supernatural confidence and does so in a manner that alludes, discreetly, to his strongly felt Marian devotion. The "smile" he can expect "as skies / Betweenpie mountains— lights a lovely mile". Norman MacKenzie's comment could hardly be bettered when he writes that in this last image

> [t]he sky itself seems to smile as the thunder clouds part to reveal a curve of vivid blue which the poet associated with the blessings of Mary. . . . The darkness of the mountains and the clouds may remain, but they are made into pied beauty by the bright sunlight between them.[134]

All in all, then, R. B. Martin is justified in finding "My own heart" "the natural culmination" of the little "sequence". The poet ends resignedly accepting of his own fallibility, and "inability to be comforted without God", but this is a God whose "radiance" will come—"not at our bidding but at His own chosen moment of revelation".[135]

---

[134] N. H. MacKenzie, *A Reader's Guide to Gerard Manley Hopkins,* 188.

[135] R. B. Martin, *Gerard Manley Hopkins,* 387.

That Nature is a Heraclitean Fire and of the comfort of the Resurrection

CLOUD-PUFFBALL, torn tufts, tossed pillows ǀ flaunt forth, then
    chevy on an air-
built thoroughfare: heaven-roysterers, in gay-gangs ǀ they
    throng; they glitter in marches.
Down roughcast, down dazzling whitewash, ǀ wherever an elm
    arches,
Shivelights and shadowtackle in long ǀ lashes lace, lance, and
    pair.
Delightfully the bright wind boisterous ǀ ropes, wrestles, beats
    earth bare
Of yestertempest's creases; ǀ in pool and rutpeel parches
Squandering ooze to squeezed ǀ dough, crust, dust; stanches,
    starches
Squadroned masks and manmarks ǀ treadmire toil there
Footfretted in it. Million-fuelèd, ǀ nature's bonfire burns on.
But quench her bonniest, dearest ǀ to her, her clearest-selvèd
    spark
Man, how fast his firedint, ǀ his mark on mind, is gone!
Both are in an unfathomable, all is in an enormous dark
Drowned. O pity and indig ǀ nation! Manshape, that shone
Sheer off, disseveral, a star, ǀ death blots black out; nor mark
        Is any of him at all so stark
But vastness blurs and time ǀ beats level. Enough! The Resur-
    rection,
A heart's-clarion! Away grief's gasping, ǀ joyless days, de-
    jection.
        Across my foundering deck shone

A beacon, an eternal beam. | Flesh fade, and mortal trash
Fall to the residuary worm; | world's wildfire, leave but ash:
            In a flash, at a trumpet crash,
I am all at once what Christ is, | since he was what I am, and
This Jack, joke, poor potsherd, | patch, matchwood, immortal
    diamond,
            Is immortal diamond.

·   ·   ·   ·   ·   ·   ·

The last poem—chronologically speaking—in this Selection comes from less than a year before Hopkins's death. It was written on 26 July 1888, which was, he noted in a letter to Canon Dixon, "a windy bright day", preceded and followed by storms of rain. After the "Terrible Sonnets", it shows a Hopkins on the way to fullest recovery, natural and supernatural alike. Its response to creation as well as to the recreating divine action of the Paschal mystery and the final consummation of all things is simply tremendous.

In the pre-Socratic fragments, the following opinion is ascribed to the philosopher Heraclitus of Miletus:

> The ordering, the same for all, no god nor man has made, but it ever was and is and will be: fire everliving, kindled in measures and in measures going out.[136]

For Heraclitus, who lived at the turn of the sixth and fifth centuries before Christ, fire is the chief clue to the character of the cosmos, the world order. Representing both "life and creativity" and "death and destruction", its property is to be "wholly transitory and always changing, while remaining

---

[136] Heraclitus, Fragment XXXVII. I follow the translation in C. H. Kahn, *The Art and Thought of Heraclitus. An Edition of the Fragments with Translation and Commentary* (Cambridge 1979), 45.

eternally the same for all".[137] Professor Charles Kahn has argued that Heraclitus found a direct parallel—expressed poetically as an identification—between fire and the sun. Commenting on *Fragment* XXXVIII, which follows immediately the Heraclitean text just quoted, Kahn writes:

> The measures by which fire is kindled and put out are to be understood as in some sense a re-enactment of the sun's regular course from solstice to solstice. And this link between the annual movements of the sun and the measured death and revival of fire is reaffirmed in the reference in [*Fragment*] XLIV to the "measures' of the sun's path as a manifestation of the divine order of the cosmos.[138]

In his view of Heraclitus's cosmogony and cosmology—his account of the coming to be and perpetuation of the world —Kahn maintains a position which, by its "pro" attitude toward the historical value of the Stoic interpretation of Heraclitus's thought, reflects the predominant conviction of nineteenth- and earlier twentieth-century scholarship. We can reasonably presume it was Hopkins's own. As the title of the poem indicates, Hopkins commits himself in some way to a Heraclitean view of the natural order. It is, as he will declare halfway through the poem's length, "nature's bonfire".

He opens, however, in a very different fashion, with a zestful—even zany—evocation of his favourite sphere of natural beauty: the sky above. Hopkins's fascination with clouds, from both the scientific and the aesthetic angles, had lasted all his adult life, as his journals bear witness. But never before had he written of them with such energy and evident pleasure. These "Cloud-puffball, torn tufts, tossed

---

137 Ibid., 138.
138 Ibid., 140.

pillows" positively "flaunt" themselves as they saunter down
the "air- / built thoroughfare". As though out with the boys
for a night on the town, they are "heaven-roysterers" who
"throng" in "gay-gangs", one of Hopkins's most successful
Anglo-Saxon-isms. Once hurled on their heavenly journey,
they "glitter in marches". But already—there is not much
time for breath in this unusually structured sonnet—Hopkins is thinking of the light they let percolate downward. It
falls along the sides of buildings, "Down roughcast, down
dazzling whitewash". It is beautifully broken up by the patterns made by the branches of trees: "wherever an elm
arches", splinters of light ("Shivelights") and mesh effects
comparable to ship's rigging ("shadowtackle") produce
delightful moving effects, or, in Hopkins's unique diction,
"lace, lance and pair". The wind, indistinguishable from the
brightness of the swirling atmosphere, behaves like a "boisterous" schoolboy, a romping prankster, as "Delightfully" it
"ropes, wrestles, beats earth bare / Of yestertempest's creases".
In puddles and rutted ground ("pool and rutpeel"), it dries
out viscous mud until the ground becomes first doughy, then
crusty, and finally dry as dust, stiffening and then turning to
powder the footprints and other marks—cart tracks? marks
left by machinery?—that man's "treadmire toil" has left
behind there.

In all this Hopkins manages to reproduce, without losing
an iota of imaginatively observed detail, the foundational
structure of the Heraclitean universe, which is characterised
by a dual movement, upward and downward: as Heraclitus
famously if gnomically exclaimed, "The way up and down
is one and the same".[139] And so it is that a cosmos that is,

---

[139] *Fragment* CIII, in the translation given by C. H. Kahn, *The Art
and Thought of Heraclitus,* 75.

in the words of the Heraclitus fragment, "fire everliving"
continues. "Million fuelèd, ⎮ nature's bonfire burns on".
Now comes the turn. What, then, Hopkins would like
to know, happens to man? Man is a part of nature. But he
is not *only* such a part. Even if he were, he would still stand
out by his qualitative distinction from all other living
things. He is "her clearest-selvèd spark". Hopkins is referring to the texture of human selfhood, to which our distinctive awareness, yours and mine, is vital. He had
annotated the *Spiritual Exercises* by writing:

> Nothing else in nature comes near this unspeakable stress
> of pitch, distinctiveness and selving, this self-being of my
> own. Nothing explains or resembles it.[140]

Man is thus the most precious manifestation of Heraclitus's
fire as he is also the most beautiful (the "bonniest"). And yet
each mortal human being vanishes like the morning-dew, or
in Hopkins's more appropriate—because duly Heraclitean—imagery, like a spark momentarily struck from flint
and as quickly extinguished. "[H]ow fast his firedint, ⎮ his
mark on mind, is gone!" Elegically, Hopkins laments the
way death "blots black out" this "star". Who can leave such
a "mark" that we can be sure it will endure in memory
through all the vicissitudes of nature's course? "[V]astness
blurs and time ⎮ beats level."

But this is a strange sort of sonnet which has a turn within
the turn. The Gospel, the faith of the Church, has at its heart
a proclamation which serves our turn—and so serves Hopkins's literary turn too, since what he is concerned with in
this poem is nothing less than the human condition *tout
court*. This utterly unexpected message rings out like a trumpet blast. "Enough! The Resurrection, / A heart's-clarion!"

---

140 *Sermons*, 123.

Hardly leaving time to explain himself, Hopkins registers at
once the reversal of the cry the thought of human mortality
had earlier wrung from him. Before we heard him cry, "O
pity and indignation!" Now the emotional tone is totally
changed: "Away grief's gasping, ǀ joyless days, dejection".
Fresh from a reading of the "Sonnets of Desolation", few
readers will suppose this exclamation easily won. What then
has happened? With the Paschal mystery, "[a]cross my
foundering deck shone / A beacon, an eternal beam". This is
a light of a new order, not the solar light whose "measures"
supplied Heraclitus with the basic rhythm of cosmic nature.
It is the light of the Resurrection of Jesus Christ, and so,
proleptically, the light of the great and general Resurrection
which Easter guarantees in the final consummatory act of
divine creative agency whose glorious anticipation it was
and is. Now Hopkins can let those processes of Heraclitean
destruction do their worst. "Flesh fade, and mortal trash /
Fall to the residuary worm; ǀ world's wildfire, leave but ash".
Instead, he looks ahead with the Paul of First Corinthians,
whose discussion of the Resurrection doctrine climaxes in
the magnificent proclamation:

> Lo! I tell you a mystery. We shall not all sleep, but we shall
> all be changed, in a moment, in the twinkling of an eye, at
> the last trumpet. (15:51–52)

"In a flash, at a trumpet crash" is Hopkins's far more dramatic version, for the divine inspiration of Scripture guarantees unsurpassable truth but not unbeatable eloquence. And
to explain the final outcome, Hopkins points to the interrelation of the doctrines of Incarnation and Resurrection. In
a marvellous exchange the Word took my humanity so that
I might share the Word incarnate's destiny beyond the order
of sin and death. "I am all at once what Christ is, ǀ since he

was what I am". And so this poor creature, a broken clay vessel, as combustible as a matchstick, this clown—"joke", "patch"—which I often am is . . . "immortal diamond": indestructible, shining, priceless. Diamonds are forever.

The Wreck of the Deutschland

PART THE FIRST

1

THOU mastering me
God! Giver of breath and bread;
World's strand, sway of the sea;
Lord of living and dead;
Thou hast bound bones and veins in me, fastened me flesh,
And after it almost unmade, what with dread,
Thy doing: and dost thou touch me afresh?
Over again I feel thy finger and find thee.

2

I did say yes
O at lightning and lashed rod;
Thou heardst me truer than tongue confess
Thy terror, O Christ, O God;
Thou knowest the walls, altar and hour and night:
The swoon of the heart that the sweep and the hurl of thee
trod
Hard down with a horror of height:
And the midriff astrain with leaning of, laced with fire of stress.

3

The frown of his face
Before me, the hurtle of hell
Behind, where, where was a, where was a place?
I whirled out wings that spell
And fled with a fling of the heart to the heart of the Host.
My heart, but you were dovewinged, I can tell,
Carrier-witted, I am bold to boast,
To flash from the flame to the flame then, tower from the grace
to the grace.

4

I am soft sift
In an hourglass—at the wall
Fast, but mined with a motion, a drift,
And it crowds, and it combs to the fall;
I steady as a water in a well, to a poise, to a pane,
But roped with, always, all the way down from the tall
Fells or flanks of the voel, a vein
Of the gospel proffer, a pressure, a principle, Christ's gift.

5

I kiss my hand
To the stars, lovely-asunder
Starlight, wafting him out of it; and
Glow, glory in thunder;
Kiss my hand to the dappled-with-damson west:
Since, tho' he is under the world's splendour and wonder,
His mystery must be instressed, stressed;
For I greet him the days I meet him, and bless when I under-
stand.

6

Not out of his bliss
    Springs the stress felt
Nor first from heaven (and few know this)
    Swings the stroke dealt—
Stroke and a stress that stars and storms deliver,
That guilt is hushed by, hearts are flushed by and melt—
    But it rides time like riding a river
(And here the faithful waver, the faithless fable and miss).

7

It dates from day
    Of his going in Galilee;
Warm-laid life of a womb-life grey;
    Manger, maiden's knee;
The dense and the driven Passion, and frightful sweat:
Thence the discharge of it, there its swelling to be,
    Though felt before, though in high flood yet—
What none would have known of it, only the heart, being hard
    at bay,

8

Is out with it! Oh,
    We lash with the best or worst
Word last! How a lush-kept plush-capped sloe
    Will, mouthed to flesh-burst,
Gush!—flush the man, the being with it, sour or sweet,
Brim, in a flash, full!—Hither then, last or first,
    To hero of Calvary, Christ's feet—
Never ask if meaning it, wanting it, warned of it—men go.

9

Be adored among men,
God, three-numberèd form;
Wring thy rebel, dogged in den,
Man's malice, with wrecking and storm.
Beyond saying sweet, past telling of tongue,
Thou art lightning and love, I found it, a winter and warm;
Father and fondler of heart thou hast wrung:
Hast thy dark descending and most art merciful then.

10

With an anvil-ding
And with fire in him forge thy will
Or rather, rather then, stealing as Spring
Through him, melt him but master him still:
Whether at once, as once at a crash Paul,
Or as Austin, a lingering-out swéet skíll,
Make mercy in all of us, out of us all
Mastery, but be adored, be adored King.

PART THE SECOND

11

'Some find me a sword; some
The flange and the rail; flame,
Fang, or flood', goes Death on drum,
And storms bugle his fame.
But wé dream we are rooted in earth—Dust!
Flesh falls within sight of us, we, though our flower the same,
Wave with the meadow, forget that there must
The sour scythe cringe, and the blear share come.

12

On Saturday sailed from Bremen,
American-outward-bound,
Take settler and seamen, take men with women,
Two hundred souls in the round—
O Father, not under thy feathers nor ever as guessing
The goal was a shoal, of a fourth the doom to be drowned;
Yet did the dark side of the bay of thy blessing
Not vault them, the millions of rounds of thy mercy not reeve
even them in?

13

Into the snows she sweeps,
Hurling the haven behind,
The Deutschland, on Sunday; and so the sky keeps,
For the infinite air is unkind,
And the sea flint-flake, black-backed in the regular blow,
Sitting Eastnortheast, in cursed quarter, the wind;
Wiry and white-fiery and whirlwind-swivellèd snow
Spins to the widow-making unchilding unfathering deeps.

14

She drove in the dark to leeward,
She struck—not a reef or a rock
But the combs of a smother of sand: night drew her
Dead to the Kentish Knock;
And she beat the bank down with her bows and the ride
of her keel;
The breakers rolled on her beam with ruinous shock;
And canvas and compass, the whorl and the wheel
Idle for ever to waft her or wind her with, these she endured.

15

Hope had grown grey hairs,
  Hope had mourning on,
Trenched with tears, carved with cares,
  Hope was twelve hours gone;
And frightful a nightfall folded rueful a day
Nor rescue, only rocket and lightship, shone,
  And lives at last were washing away:
To the shrouds they took,—they shook in the hurling and
  horrible airs.

16

One stirred from the rigging to save
  The wild woman-kind below,
With a rope's end round the man, handy and brave—
  He was pitched to his death at a blow,
For all his dreadnought breast and braids of thew:
They could tell him for hours, dandled the to and fro
  Through the cobbled foam-fleece. What could he do
With the burl of the fountains of air, buck and the flood of
  the wave?

17

They fought with God's cold—
  And they could not and fell to the deck
(Crushed them) or water (and drowned them) or rolled
  With the sea-romp over the wreck.
Night roared, with the heart-break hearing a heart-broke rabble,
The woman's wailing, the crying of child without check—
  Till a lioness arose breasting the babble,
A prophetess towered in the tumult, a virginal tongue told.

18

Ah, touched in your bower of bone,
　　Are you! turned for an exquisite smart,
　Have you! make words break from me here all alone,
　　Do you!—mother of being in me, heart.
O unteachably after evil, but uttering truth,
　Why, tears! is it? tears; such a melting, a madrigal start!
　　Never-eldering revel and river of youth,
What can it be, this glee? the good you have there of your own?

19

Sister, a sister calling
　　A master, her master and mine!—
　And the inboard seas run swirling and hawling;
　　The rash smart sloggering brine
Blinds her; but she that weather sees one thing, one;
　Has one fetch in her: she rears herself to divine
　　Ears, and the call of the tall nun
To the men in the tops and the tackle rode over the
　　storm's brawling.

20

She was the first of a five and came
　　Of a coifèd sisterhood.
　(O Deutschland, double a desperate name!
　　O world wide of its good!
But Gertrude, lily, and Luther, are two of a town,
　Christ's lily and beast of the waste wood:
　　From life's dawn it is drawn down,
Abel is Cain's brother and breasts they have sucked the same.)

21

Loathed for a love men knew in them,
    Banned by the land of their birth,
    Rhine refused them, Thames would ruin them;
        Surf, snow, river and earth
Gnashed. but thou art above, thou Orion of light;
    Thy unchancelling poising palms were weighing the worth,
        Thou martyr-master: in thy sight
Storm flakes were scroll-leaved flowers, lily showers—sweet
    heaven was astrew in them.

22

Five! the finding and sake
    And cipher of suffering Christ.
    Mark, the mark is of man's make
        And the word of it Sacrificed.
But he scores it in scarlet himself on his own bespoken,
Before-time-taken, dearest prizèd and priced—
    Stigma, signal, cinquefoil token
For lettering of the lamb's fleece, ruddying of the rose-flake.

23

Joy fall to thee, father Francis,
    Drawn to the Life that died;
    With the gnarls of the nails in thee, niche of the lance, his
        Lovescape crucified.
And seal of his seraph-arrival! and these thy daughters
And five-livèd and leavèd favour and pride,
    Are sisterly sealed in wild waters,
To bathe in his fall-gold mercies, to breathe in his all-fire
    glances.

24

Away in the loveable west,
   On a pastoral forehead of Wales,
I was under a roof, I was at rest,
   And they the prey of the gales;
She to the black-about air, to the breaker, the thickly
Falling flakes, to the throng that catches and quails
   Was calling 'O Christ, Christ, come quickly';
The cross to her she calls Christ to her, christens her wild-worst
   Best.

25

The majesty! what did she mean?
   Breathe, arch and original Breath.
Is it love in her of the being as her lover had been?
   Breathe, body of lovely Death.
They were else-minded then, altogether, the men
Woke thee with a *We are perishing* in the weather of Gen-
   nesareth.
   Or is it that she cried for the crown then,
The keener to come at the comfort for feeling the combating
   keen?

26

For how to the heart's cheering
   The down-dugged ground-hugged grey
Hovers off, the jay-blue heavens appearing
   Of pied and peeled May!
Blue-beating and hoary-glow height; or night, still higher,
With belled fire and the moth-soft Milky Way,
   What by your measure is the heaven of desire,
The treasure never eyesight got, nor was ever guessed what for
   the hearing?

27

No, but it was not these.
The jading and jar of the cart,
Time's tasking, it is fathers that asking for ease
Of the sodden-with-its-sorrowing heart,
Not danger, electrical horror; then further it finds
The appealing of the Passion is tenderer in prayer apart:
Other, I gather, in measure her mind's
Burden, in wind's burly and beat of endragonèd seas.

28

But how shall I . . . make me room there:
Reach me a . . . Fancy, come faster—
Strike you the sight of it? look at it loom there,
Thing that she . . . There then! the Master,
Ipse, the only one, Christ, King, Head:
He was to cure the extremity where he had cast her;
Do, deal, lord it with living and dead;
Let him ride, her pride, in his triumph, despatch and have done
with his doom there.

29

Ah! there was a heart right!
There was single eye!
Read the unshapeable shock night
And knew the who and the why;
Wording it how but by him that present and past,
Heaven and earth are word of, worded by?—
The Simon Peter of a soul! to the blast
Tarpeïan-fast, but a blown beacon of light.

30

Jesu, heart's light,
Jesu, maid's son,
What was the feast followed this night
Thou hadst glory of this nun?—
Feast of the one woman without stain.
For so conceivèd, so to conceive thee is done;
But here was heart-throe, birth of a brain,
Word, that heard and kept thee and uttered thee outright.

31

Well, she has thee for the pain, for the
Patience; but pity of the rest of them!
Heart, go and bleed at a bitterer vein for the
Comfortless unconfessed of them—
No not uncomforted: lovely-felicitous Providence
Finger of a tender of, O of a feathery delicacy, the breast of the
Maiden could obey do, be a bell to, ring of it, and
Startle the poor sheep back! is the shipwreck than a harvest,
does tempest carry the grain for thee?

32

I admire thee, master of the tides,
Of the Yore-flood, of the year's fall;
The recurb and the recovery of the gulf's sides,
The girth of it and the wharf of it and the wall;
Stanching, quenching ocean of a motionable mind;
Ground of being, and granite of it: past all
Grasp God, throned behind
Death with a sovereignty that heeds but hides, bodes but abides;

33

With a mercy that outrides
The all of water, an ark
For the listener; for the lingerer with a love glides
Lower than death and the dark;
A vein for the visiting of the past-prayer, pent in prison
The-last-breath-penitent spirits—the uttermost mark
Our passion-plungèd giant risen,
The Christ of the Father compassionate, fetched in the storm
of his strides.

34

Now burn, new born to the world,
Double-naturèd name,
The heaven-flung, heart-fleshed, maiden-furled
Miracle-in-Mary-of-flame,
Mid-numberèd he in three of the thunder-throne!
Not a dooms-day dazzle in his coming nor dark as he
came;
Kind, but royally reclaiming his own;
A released shower, let flash to the shire, not a lightning of fire
hard-hurled.

35

Dame, at our door
Drowned, and among our shoals,
Remember us in the roads, the heaven-haven of the
reward:
Our King back, Oh, upon English souls!
Let him easter in us, be a dayspring to the dimness of us,
be a crimson-cresseted east,
More brightening her, rare-dear Britain, as his reign rolls,
Pride, rose, prince, hero of us, high-priest,
Our hearts' charity's hearth's fire, our thoughts' chivalry's
throng's Lord.

.   .   .   .

Once read or heard, studied and appropriated, never forgotten. This is the unforgettable poem, searing, its effect enduring, that broke Hopkins's long poetic silence. I place it at the end because it is certainly the longest and very probably the most difficult poem in Hopkins's oeuvre. So as not to lose new readers' sympathy, it seemed advisable to approach it by way of others. "The Wreck of the Deutschland" is also, I believe, Hopkins's greatest work, and so, adapting the words of the steward at the Marriage Feast at Cana, we have kept the best wine till the end (cf. John 2:10).

The circumstances of the writing of "The Wreck of the Deutschland" have already been touched on in the Introduction. Let it suffice to say, then, how moved Hopkins was by the newspaper reports of the sinking of this vessel, whose victims included Franciscan nursing sisters exiled from Germany by the anti-Church legislation of the 1870s.[141] His fascination with sailing and shipwreck, derived from his father's profession; his awe before the power of nature; his pity for fellow-creatures in extremity; his never-flagging Catholic zeal and piety: all these powerful motivations came together to make possible, in consort with his verbal brilliance, craftsmanship, and high originality, what he called this "ode".

The word "ode" gives us an important clue. In a sense to be defined, Hopkins's model was one of the early Greek poets he had studied at Oxford, Pindar. In his own—abortive—work on the Greek poets, Hopkins had noted the presence in their verse of "two strains of thought running together and like counterpointed": The "overthought" which "everybody" can see, but also an

---

[141] For a concise account of the circumstances of the wreck, drawing on materials outside the poem, see N. H. MacKenzie, *A Reader's Guide to Gerard Manley Hopkins,* 29–33.

underthought, conveyed chiefly in the choice of metaphors, etc. used and often only half realized by the poet himself, not necessarily having any connection with the subject in hand but usually having a connection and suggested by some circumstance of the scene or of the story.[142]

Later critical writing has tended to confirm the accuracy of this insight, notably for the Pindaric odes, where, as the work of Gilbert Norwood tends to demonstrate, an unstated key will frequently be found to bring together disparate images and themes.[143] So likewise with "The Wreck of the Deutschland", whose obscure principles of organisation and peculiar use of metaphor led Robert Bridges to enter his caveat to readers: This poem was a "dragon before the gates". "Never again", wrote the American critic Todd Bender, would Hopkins go "to such lengths in non-logical structure, disjunctive diction, or far-fetched imagery".[144] And yet, if we adopt a "Pindaric" approach to this "dragon", we can lay it in its lair. The "underthought", unifying the poem and its disparate strands of imagery, is, Bender proposes:

> [t]he wild water [which] manifests the awesome power of God, at once cruel and kind, destroying the life of the nuns but bringing them to Heaven . . .—the grace and power of God, bringing physical death but eternal life, manifest and symbolized in water.[145]

It will almost certainly be helpful to bear this thought in mind throughout. The editor of the first of the fully schol-

---

142 *Further Letters*, 252.

143 G. Norwood, *Pindar* (Berkeley, CA 1945). This "new doctrine", claimed Norwood, "reveals the whole poem as a unified work of art", ibid., 80.

144 T. K. Bender, *Gerard Manley Hopkins. The Classical Background and Critical Reception of His Work* (Baltimore, MD 1966), 9.

145 Ibid., 86.

arly editions, W. H. Gardner, identified the main divisions of the poem as follows: "Part the First", consisting of stanzas 1–10: a "meditation on God's infinite power and masterhood'; "Part the Second", subdivided as stanzas 11–17a: a narrative of the shipwreck; stanzas 17b–31: the voice of the nun calling above the tumult; stanzas 32–35: an act of adoration of God's majesty and inscrutable wisdom.[146] In these four sections the poem unfolds its disclosure of God's power and mercy made manifest in water.

> First, the poet himself, converted, is filled with God's mercy like water in a well as his physical life runs out. Second, the passengers of the Deutschland who drown see only the terrible power of God in the destructive water. Third, the nun too sees the awful power, but in her extremity realizes that God is harvesting her by means of the water, that her death is taking her to God's Heavenhaven. Finally, the English have wilfully deprived themselves of the water of faith and the poet prays that God will shower His mercy on the nation before it is too late.[147]

Part the First

The ode's opening is exceedingly impressive. It addresses God as the *mysterium tremendum et fascinosum*, "the fearful and wonderful Mystery" behind all phenomena, and—more than this—in language redolent of the Hebrew prophets, the Creator of all things and the Providence which rules them. The awe-struck exclamation—"Thou mastering me / God!'—initiates the grave rhythm of this stanza which has

---

[146] W. H. Gardner, *Poems of Gerard Manley Hopkins* (London 1948, 3rd edition), 220–21.

[147] Ibid., 94–95. Bender points out how much of the poem's imagery is taken from liquids of various kinds, as different as sweat and the juice gushing from burst fruit.

been compared to the solemn tolling of a bell.[148] God is not only the Maker and Provider, "Giver of breath and bread", which might simply be reassuring or even domestic. He is also the absolute Limit where everything created confronts the Abyss ('World's strand') and the Ruler of the vast oceans whose surging waters he alone can "sway". As "Lord of living and dead", he is sovereign over all human beings—and Hopkins will shortly explore what this means in his own case. But the title of the poem may alert the reader to more immediate consequences: His rule comprehends the vital forces of nature to which the *Deutschland* succumbed, and the souls of the drowned. Hopkins shudders at the thought of this dread divine mastery, which is not only creative, "Thou hast bound bones and veins in me, fastened me flesh", but also potentially destructive, "And after it almost unmade, what with dread, / Thy doing". Is this God, then, the Lord God of Israel, the Father of our Lord Jesus Christ, or does the Holy Mystery shows its visage as Shiva the Destroyer? Hopkins knows his Scripture and doctrine well enough to be clear what he is saying. Creation and the Providence that conserves it govern a world where things do not only come into being. They also pass out of it again in a transience which belongs with the divine decrees and, indeed, with the divine Wisdom. Moreover, there is also the special providence of God in dealings with human beings, who may need to experience a dying to self before they can live to him. Hopkins experiences renewed encounter with the God who smites or, at the very least, probes, so as ultimately to heal and transform. "[A]nd dost thou touch me afresh? / Over again I feel thy finger and find thee." Until these last two lines, were the stanza to have an iconic equiv-

---

[148] D. McChesney, *A Hopkins Commentary,* 36.

alent it would be a Byzantine *Pantokrator*. Now it is surely
Michelangelo's Sistine Chapel *Creation*.

If the Pindaresque "underthought" of "The Wreck of the
Deutschland" is the stormy waters of divine agency, at once
negative and ultra-positive, the second and third stanzas of
Part the First, which tell of Hopkins's fundamental voca-
tional decision, may be said already to anticipate the shipwreck scenes which will follow in Part the Second. He had
said "yes" to this almighty Lord, said it "at lightning and
lashed rod", as though he were an indentured man on a gal-
ley, under a hard taskmaster in a tempest when the elements
were raging. Though only his heart spoke, what the divine
Christ—divine in his hypostasis, divine in the nature con-
substantial with the Father—heard was a speech "truer than
tongue". And that speech confessed his fearful majesty,
"Thy terror". No Jesus meek and mild can be named here if
the crucified and risen One really is one being with the Lord
of all.

And now the retrospect becomes more narratively specific. "Thou knowest the walls, altar and hour and night"
where this confession was made. A vigil, then, in some
church or chapel, and the most likely locale is the chapel of
the Jesuit novitiate in Richmond Park, the occasion a night
some time in Eastertide 1868, when he made the retreat
whereby he decided to become a priest and religious.[149]
Hopkins recaptures for himself, and for us, the strain of
this "existential decision"—for once the jargon of that mid-
twentieth-century philosophical movement seems entirely
fitting. It happened not in some solipsistic reverie but in
almost physical consciousness of the pressing invitation of
the God of grace, frightening in its urgency. After this

---

[149] Suggestive evidence based on stanzas 2 and 3 of the poem is laid
out in J. F. Cotter, *Inscape,* 26–30.

"swoon of the heart" under the impact of the "sweep and the hurl of thee" Hopkins felt a sense of the weight of God (the Hebrews called it *kabod*, Augustine *pondus*) bearing on him from a vertiginous height. Stanza 2 ends by registering the muscular tension of this moment of definitive commitment: "The midriff astrain with leaning of, laced with fire of stress".

Actually, this is only a pause, because stanza 3 resumes the account of this costing commitment. Hopkins knew that the fear of the Lord is a biblical and theological prerequisite for appropriate love of him. The true God is leonine rather than feline. His Word is, as the writer to the Hebrews affirms:

> sharper than any two-edged sword, piercing to the division of soul and spirit, of joints and marrow, and discerning the thoughts and intentions of the heart (4:12).

Obedience to that Word is not, for our personal destiny, a bagatelle. In his essay "On Personality, Grace and Free Will", Hopkins wrote on this subject with massive sobriety.

> [T]here must be something which shall truly be the creature's in the work of corresponding with grace: this is the *arbitrium*, the verdict on God's side, the saying Yes, the 'doing-agree' (to speak barbarously), and looked at in itself such a nothing is the creature before its creator, it is to be found no more than the mere wish, discernible by God's eyes, that it might do as he wishes, might correspond, might say Yes to him; correspondence itself in on man's side not so much corresponding as the wish to correspond, and this least sigh of desire, this one aspiration, is the life and spirit of man.[150]

---

150 *Sermons*, 154–55.

Hopkins took very seriously the doctrine of Hell as the outcome of voluntary, conscious rejection of the Will of God,
a will that, if we follow it, is also—in the words of Dante—
"our peace". In the same essay he added:

> [T]his sigh or aspiration or stirring of the spirit towards
> God is a *forestall* of the thing to be done. . . . And by this
> infinitesimal act the creature does what in it lies to bridge
> the gulf between its present actual and worser pitch of will
> and its future better one.[151]

To know how one's own will is situated vis-à-vis the Will of
God is far more significant than giving compass readings
for our geographical location. "The frown of his face /
Before me, the hurtle of hell / Behind, where, where was a,
where was a place?"

In point of fact, by grace, cooperating with his own freedom, Hopkins had given a generous response to the divine
demand. Like a homing pigeon, he had "whirled out wings",
and "fled with a fling of the heart" to answer the heart that
had spoken to him, at "the heart of the Host". There is an
extraordinary density of devotional meaning packed into
these last few words. The "Sacred Heart" of Jesus, a devotional *topos* especially favoured by the Society for its connexion with a generous soteriology—the maximalisation of God's
effective will to save—bears an intimate relation to the mystery of the Holy Eucharist, the sacrament of Christ's opened
heart on the Cross. The Hopkins of whom, as the stanza
opens, we might suspect a self-depreciating, negative, and
sub-Christian spirituality, now positively congratulates himself on what, under the grace of the Holy Spirit, the Heavenly
Dove, he has been able of himself to perform. "My heart,
but you were dovewinged, I can tell, / Carrier-witted." He

---

[151] Ibid., 155.

admits in a brazen fashion St Paul would approve, "I am bold to boast". This is no grovelling human worm, but a Christian man exercising his *parrhesia*, or right of free speech, before the Lord. He *did* "flash from the flame to the flame" in that moment, or, in another less metaphorical image, "tower from the grace to the grace". In the essay "On Personality, Grace and Free Will" just cited, Hopkins describes "elevating grace" as lifting "the receiver from one cleave of being to another and to a vital act in Christ . . . , the aspiration in answer to his inspiration".[152] James Finn Cotter, the most theologically minded of Hopkins's critics, ties this statement to the third stanza of "The Wreck of the Deutschland", remarking how

> Hopkins mounts from the flame and grace of Christ's inspiration to the flame and grace of his own aspiration. . . . When love quickens, heart answers to heart.[153]

Even so, the fourth and fifth stanzas are considerably softer in tone, but once again aquatic imagery is to the fore, warning us of the ambivalence of divine action which is at once judgment and grace. Hopkins is conscious of what Norman MacKenzie calls his "friable mortality", an excellent conceptual equivalent for the poet's imagistic "soft sift / In an hourglass". He sees his little craft moored by some sea wall, where the unpredictable waters make it "mined with a motion", the tide raising and lowering it, as the water level "crowds, and . . . combs to a fall". Not much security here. Now, however, the nautical scene fades and a landscape with a well flanked by hillsides takes its place. Almost certainly Hopkins

---

[152] *Sermons*, 156.

[153] J. F. Cotter, *Inscape*, 28–29. Cotter repeats his own closing words in Latin, to connect Hopkins with Newman's cardinalatial motto. This is a pleasing thought, given Newman's spiritual fatherhood of the poet, but Newman did not become a cardinal until four years after the poem was written.

was thinking of his beloved St Winefred's Well, a favourite walk of his from St Beuno's. Like the well-water there, Hopkins can keep his level, but that is only because his resources, as those of the well, are constantly renewed by a stream: not the silver trickles running down the voel, the Welsh hillside, their strands gradually converging into a "rope" of water near the foot of the mountain, but the grace of Christ to whom the poet is "roped" through the apostolic succession, the apostolic Tradition, of the Church. This life-giving spiritual water is at first an offer, then an effective presence in our lives, and finally—if we cooperate with it fully—the animating force behind everything we are and do: "[A] vein / Of the gospel proffer, a pressure, a principle". At none of these stages does it ever become, however, *merely* ours. It never loses its character as donation. It is always "Christ's gift".

The fifth stanza shows us the quintessential Hopkins of the nature poems which in two years' time he will start to write. Here the softening of tone I mentioned becomes lovely, lyrical. On an evening bright with the emerging stars, when as sun sets the skies in the west are purple-streaked, "dappled-with-damson", Hopkins is in the habit of "kissing his hand" to Christ whom all this beauty makes visible as the Love behind the world. The Lord is present "under the world's splendour and wonder", but this "mystery", a mystery of the externalisation of the Infinite in the finite, must be "instressed, stressed". That is: it must be clarified in its proper pattern and its energies proclaimed.

> The first intention . . . of God outside himself or, as they say, *ad extra,* outwards, the first outstress of God's power was Christ. . . . Why did the Son of God go thus forth from the Father not only in the eternal and intrinsic procession of the Trinity but also by an extrinsic and less than eternal, let us say aeonian one?—To give God glory and

that by sacrifice.[154]

These are deep things, but insight comes, through responsiveness to the Lord in prayer and by intelligence, receptive to illumining grace. "For I greet him the days I meet him, and bless when I understand."

Insight received brings it about that, in the poem's next three stanzas, the mood abruptly changes. The "stress felt" that corresponds to Hopkins's subject—tragedy at sea—is not simply the divine creative action through the Word. The "stress" concerned does not spring "out of his bliss" nor "first from heaven . . . / Swings the stroke dealt". When Hopkins adds that "few know this", we are warned that a major theological disclosure is in view. Stanzas 6, 7, and 8 are dominated by the thought of the Passion of the incarnate Christ and its positively cosmic implications, since this was the suffering and death of the One through whom, in, whom, and for whom the world was made. The "stress that stars and storms deliver"—here the beauty and the terror of nature are bracketed together—is not simply the divine creativity. It is something more dreadful, but also more marvellous still: the divine redemptive action, prefigured from the beginning of the world, though only fully realised on Calvary. *Christ's atoning work* is what "guilt is hushed by, hearts are flushed by and melt"—something on which Catholics and Evangelicals could agree in Victorian England. Not for nothing was Westminster Cathedral, the flagship of the English Catholic Church, "The Metropolitan Cathedral *of the Precious Blood*".[155] The Atonement was in time but, granted the divine as well as human nature of the One who suffered for us, time does not confine it. Rather, it

---

154 *Sermons,* 197.
155 The Neo-Byzantine fabric was not constructed until the years 1895–1903, but the site was acquired, and plans begun, as early

"rides time like riding a river", ever present and active in its flow. As Hopkins recognised, this supra-temporal enduring of the effects of the Passion of the Incarnate One neither is well understood by the faithful nor—hardly surprisingly—does it ever enter an agnostic's mind. It remains nonetheless the single most important truth about the world. A universally pertinent truth, then, but also a contingent fact, and, accordingly dateable. "It dates from day / Of his going in Galilee", and, so stanza 7 has it, from the momentous slice of time that joins the Annunciation (and therefore the Incarnation) to the Resurrection (and thus Christ's entire Paschal Mystery). Without blessed Mary's consent, and her nurture of this Child, his saving Sacrifice could never have been possible, which is why a theologically admirable late medieval iconography in the west portrays the Cross as a lily-tree.[156] Hopkins has his own manner of insinuating this connexion, and it lies in the ambivalence of the poem's next line, which reads: "Warm-laid grave of a womb-life grey". In one way, those words refer to the Incarnation. In Mary's confinement, the Lord himself is even more confined *secundum humanitatem,* "according to his humanity". Intra-uterine existence is grey indeed for One who, in his divinity, moves the sun and the other stars. And though in the sheltering care of Mary's heart as well as body he is welcomed cordially, *warmly,* into the created world, he has come in order to die in a far stronger sense than any ordinary mortal. The swaddling clothes of the babe in the

as 1867: see B. Little, *Catholic Churches since 1623. A Study of Roman Catholic Churches in England and Wales from Penal Times to the Present Decade* (London 1966), 167–72.

156 For a splendid contemporary theological account of this connexion, see J. Saward, *The Mysteries of March: Hans Urs von Balthasar on the Incarnation and Easter* (London 1990).

manger, on the "maiden's knee", are prophetic of the winding-sheet of his tomb. And in another way, indeed, this line of the ode has in view that tomb and the new life that sprang from there. The holy sepulchre, the grave of Christ, was more truly the grave of that "womb-life grey", which is what existence is for the rest of us, half-alive as we are most of the time, and in any case, living only a natural existence not up to our intended measure. His grave proved "warm-laid" to our stupendous benefit, since from it the ever-pulsating supernatural as well as natural life of the Risen One emerged on the first Easter Day.

Only Atonement makes Resurrection possible. The energies of the new life of Easter are generated on the Cross. "The dense and the driven Passion, and frightful sweat" is the source of the "discharge", the "swelling". In a later meditation Hopkins wrote:

> The piercing of Christ's side. The sacred body and the sacred heart seemed waiting for an opportunity of discharging themselves and testifying their total devotion of themselves to the cause of man.[157]

Prefigured, no doubt, in the Old Testament ("Though felt before") and still "in high flood", since the flow of saving grace continues not least through the Mass which is the perpetual efficacious sign of Christ's sacrifice in the Church, nevertheless "none would have known" of this tremendous Lover had not his blood flowed on the hill, whence it streams for ever through the firmament.

Stanza 8 is dominated by the daring image of the sloe: *prunus spinosa*—a wild plum growing on blackthorn. William Cobbett in his 1825 essay *The Woodlands* wrote:

---

[157] *Sermons,* 255.

Everyone knows that this is a Thorn of the Plum kind; that it bears very small black plums which are called Sloes, which have served love-song poets in all ages with a simile whereby to describe the eyes of their beauties. . . . These beauty-describing sloes have a little plum-like pulp . . . which . . . is astringent beyond the powers of alum. The juice expressed from this pulp is of a greenish black, and mixed with water, in which a due proportion of logwood has been steeped, receiving, in addition, a sufficient proportion of cheap French brandy, makes the finest Port wine in the world.[158]

It is a juice capable, then, of bitterness and sweetness alike. The Christ who came in the ripeness of time—a "lush-kept, plush-capped sloe"—was, as it were, bitten until his flesh was pierced. And from that "flesh-burst" gushed his redeeming grace, flushing those who "mouthed" it, and striking them as either (in Cobbett's word) "astringent" or so much the contrary as to suggest the sweetest wines. *Which* of these, "sour or sweet", it is depends, in the countryside, on whether frost has mellowed the fruit. In the realm of the human spirit, how we experience that taste will turn, rather, on what our deepest aspirations are. Hopkins, as befits a member of an anti-Jansenist order, believed that people will come to Christ the Fount of life albeit belatedly. Even without wishing to, they will be drawn to the "hero of Calvary, Christ,'s feet". "Hither then, last or first, . . . / Never ask if meaning it, wanting it, warned of it—men go". Congruently, then, the remaining two stanzas of Part the First will speak not of the contrasting situations of those who are on the way to salvation and those who are perishing, but of the two contrasting aspects of God's action in Everyman's regard: judging and redeeming, testing and saving. These apply to great sinners, and great saints.

---

[158] Cited in R. Mabey, *Flora Britannica,* 197.

Stanza 9 opens with a mighty acclamation of the divine Trinity: "Be adored among men, / God, three-numberèd form". Overall, this stanza insists that the negative features of divine agency are functionally ordered to the revelation of their positive counterparts. Hopkins calls on the dread Master to do his worst with man: "Wring thy rebel, dogged in den, / Man's malice, with wrecking and storm". In the context of the disaster that overtook the *Deutschland* one might think the last image quite singularly insensitive. But our discomfort is intended, and its meaning will soon become plain. If God cannot be encompassed in language ("past telling of tongue") that is, above all, owing to his ultra-positivity ("Beyond saying sweet"). So when Hopkins appears to balance nicely the divine economic attributes, God's qualities in our regard—"Thou art lightning and love, . . . a winter and warm", this is not because the divine being is polarised between good and evil, after the fashion C. G. Jung suggested in his *Answer to Job*. No, it is because God knows how to love human beings in such wise that they can come to their own salvation, their beatitude. He is the "Father and fondler" of the hearts he has "wrung". When his "dark" is "descending" on us, this is not the manifestation of some hateful shadow-side but the contrary. "[Thou] most art merciful then."

So Hopkins is yielding to no sadistic impulse when he calls on God, at the opening of stanza 10, to beat people like a blacksmith forges the iron shoe of the horse—an action altogether to the horse's favour. But he can also hope that God will be able to achieve their final good by gentler methods, as spring "steal[s]" through nature, revivifying it gently, imperceptibly. Such a method would "melt" man, but it would "master" him nevertheless, and that is the really important thing—and why the harsher treatment of the divine Vulcan in his forge is also quite legitimate in Hopkins's eyes. This process of conversion could be instantaneous, like St Paul's on the Damascus Road which was "at a crash", a phrase that indicates not only suddenness but also violence. Or it might be long drawn out, subtle and delicate, as St Augustine's in its various stages at Carthage, Milan, Rome, Thagaste: a "lingering-out swéet skíll". All that matters in the end is that God "Make mercy in all of us": that he may communicate his grace in such a way that we not only receive his mercy but have it intrinsically within us—and therefore can begin to transmit it to others. The *Oratio dominicalis* Hopkins prayed every day in the Mass and Office says, "Forgive us our trespasses as we forgive those that trespass against us", and this is always a prospective prayer. Just so the divine "Mastery" shows itself. Part the First of the ode does not want to finish in anthropocentricity, however. So, however things befall: "be adored, be adored King".

Part the Second

Part the First had opened with the poet, in MacKenzie's words, "finding the eternal God".[159] By contrast, Part the Second, the critic continues, begins with a far more common scenario in everyday life, people finding his instrument, death. Like an adjutant to a medieval herald, Death, suitably personified, bangs his drum while bugles blow. His message is stark yet colourfully dramatic, as he enumerates the various instruments in his armoury by which mortals can die. Possibly, as has been suggested, Hopkins had in mind one of the fascinating but rather horrific late medieval frescoes of the "Dance of Death", such as the especially well-preserved sequence on the covered bridge over the Reuss at Lucerne.

---

[159] N. H. MacKenzie, *A Reader's Guide to Gerard Manley Hopkins,* 38.

But Hopkins's examples of death-traps encompass modern as well as ancient: railway accidents ("The flange and the rail") as well as "flame, / Fang, or flood". If in the richly textured Christological poetry which prevailed in the last stanzas of Part the First we have lost sight of the chaos waters on which the *Deutschland* foundered, Hopkins refocusses our attention by having "storms" do the bugling for Death's fame. The trouble is that, despite the victories Death notches up in others, each man lives as though he were not mortal. We think we are rooted in the earth, like some immemorial oak. But while we are right that we are of the earth that is because we are "—Dust!". Even when "Flesh falls within sight of us", when we actually observe the death rattle or the tragic accident on the Liverpool to Manchester railway, we still imagine that we shall continue to bloom indefinitely, like flowers that "Wave with the meadow". But the "sour" reaper whose scythe makes fieldmice and other tiny earth creatures "cringe", whose ploughshare "blear" (blind and therefore undiscriminating) overturns the meadowland and whatever is on it, he is coming for each one of us.

Stanza 12 begins the narrative section of the poem by telling of how death befell in one case in a misadventure with many casualties. The *Deutschland* left Bremerhaven (on 4 December 1875), bound for the United States of America at a time of fairly large-scale German emigration. The Franciscan nuns were exceptional in that, though they were bound for an American apostolate, that was simply because the belief of Prussians that Germany's unity lay in a national cultural Protestantism had forced them out. In tallying the numbers on board, accordingly, Hopkins omits them even though they—and especially one of them—will be the heroine of the piece. Women plus men, settlers plus seamen, the total complement was around two hundred. (Hopkins refers

not to "people" but to "souls", thereby alerting us to the
theme of death and judgment which will preoccupy him.)
There was no reason to think the company had especially
entrusted themselves to divine protection on this voyage. At
any rate, without the divine concursus in the operation of
secondary causes all other factors favouring a prosperous
journey were of no avail. They were not, it would seem,
under the Father's "feathers". "Wings" was and is the more
customary rendering of Psalm 91:4, but the poet, used as a
Catholic priest to reciting the Psalms in Latin, probably
thought of the English translation by Coverdale as found in
the *Book of Common Prayer*, which was familiar to him from
his Anglican upbringing. Their de facto goal would not be,
as they assumed, New York, where they were meant to dock,
nor even Southampton where the ship would call in. No,
"The goal was a shoal", and the somewhat childish internal
rhyme serves to bring out the macabre disparity between
expectations and what transpired. A quarter of those on the
Deutschland would perish, and Hopkins brings it home to us
that there is no comedy here. The "doom" that a "fourth"
would meet is not only the nautical disaster but the day of
God's judgment, anticipated as that was for each one who
met death in that hour. Hopkins's conviction that God is terrible only to be wonderful, that he smites only so as to save,
now supervenes. Even in that awful hour, "the dark side of
the bay of [God's] blessing" rounded them like the heavenly
"vault" above. Using a shipping metaphor, he is sure that the
divine mercy in its plenitude—its "million of rounds"—
"reeve[d]" them in: The comparison is with a sailor pulling a
rope through a hole in a block to make it secure.[160]

Stanza 13 wonderfully evokes the chill voyage on a wintry
sea. The violent action-words for the ship's movement—the

---

[160] J. Milroy, *The Language of Gerard Manley Hopkins*, 243.

192 • HOPKINS: THEOLOGIAN'S POET

Deutschland "sweeps" into the snow, "hurling" the harbour behind her—reminds the reader who had followed the results of the official enquiry how the vessel was moving far too fast for the weather conditions. Hopkins graphically sums up what these conditions were. "[T]he infinite air was unkind": in fact, blowing from a "cursed quarter" (east-northeast), the wind would drive the ship off its course toward the west, with the result that it struck the shoals off the Thames estuary. But the "unkindness" in question has a further dimension. Originally, the word "kind" meant "having to do with one's kin" or "congruent with one's nature". (The prayers beginning "O kind Jesu" in the medieval primers were supplications to one who was in human nature and therefore our "kin".) But on the *Deutschland*'s North Sea crossing, the cosmic elements appeared to have changed from their nature, and very much to the worse. The sea had become "flint-flake" and "black-backed", harsher and more hostile to man than we should expect from the element of water. The snow, "whirlwind swivellèd", was barely recognisable, "wiry", as it fell in hurtful coils, and "white-fiery", as destructive to those exposed to it as white-hot heat would be. And always beneath the fated vessel were the fathomless waters that were going to make women widows just as they would also render fathers childless and children fatherless. The chaos waters of the deep, which for the Hebrew Bible are the foil and potentially the antithesis of God's creative work, parody that creativity by their "widow-making" force. But really of course, despite the positivity of the verb "to make", this is all unmaking, as the succeeding epithets "unchilding" and "unfathering" make plain.

Stanza 14 chronicles the moment of disaster. "[N]ight drew her / Dead to the Kentish Knock", a ridged sandbank notoriously perilous to shipping, some twenty-three miles east of Harwich. Such was the poor seamanship of her cap-

tain that the *Deutschland* made as if straight for the instrument of her wrecking, "dead on" target for it. And so she
was fatally stricken, "dead", in far more grievous a sense.
Caught on the ridges—the "combs"—of the murderous
sandbanks ("a smother of sand" conveys an appropriately
felonious feel), she had no option but to "endure" the
repeated smashing of the "breakers", the waves, until she
was herself broken. Neither the ship's machinery—pro-
peller ("whorl") and wheel, nor the accoutrements of sailing, the "canvas and compass", could do a thing to save her.

In stanza 15 the human cargo awaits—with foreboding.
As the stanza opens, rhythm and diction conspire to shape
an atmosphere which only too accurately indicates what lies
ahead at its end. Hopkins paints a ghastly figure of hope as
an old crone, her visage furrowed by anxiety and weeping,
and already wearing her funeral weeds. Nor did the coming
of night, the time of recuperative sleep, do anything to heal
that appalling day of waiting for a rescue that never came.
Contemporary accounts describe how the *Deutschland*'s
plight was noticed by lightships, but they could not have
reached her without endangering their own crews. (Those
stranded believed, wrongly, that the reason was callous-
ness.)[161] Hopkins contrasts the wonderful lightening of spirits that salvaging passengers and crew would have brought
with the fitful and, in the event, pointless lighting of distant
flares. And so it was that "frightful a nightfall folded rueful a
day". As the stanza closes, the funeral atmosphere turns
finally into actual death, as the first victims meet their end by
being washed overboard. Some, trying to escape the enormous waves, climbed up into the ship's rigging, which, however, only served them as "shrouds". The canvas sails would
be their funeral cerements.

---

[161] N. H. MacKenzie, *A Reader's Guide to Gerard Manley Hopkins,* 31.

In stanza 16 Hopkins recounts, with discretion, one especially horrible moment when a seaman, poised on one of the ship's masts, attempted to save a woman on deck by roping himself and swinging down to pick her up. Under the impact of the wind and water he was dashed against the ship's side and decapitated, though his headless body remained in the rigging swinging "to and fro". Hopkins, with his usual admiration for physical courage and sheer strength, contrasts the man's "dreadnought breast and braids of thew" with his appalling end when like a child's plaything he is "dandled . . . [t]hrough the . . . foam-fleece", the softness of this description of the snow suggestive of a child's nursery and adding by dint of contrast to the brutality of the death. The chief contrast, however, remains that between man in his vulnerability and the might of nature: "What could he do / With the burl of the fountains of air, buck and the flood of the wave?" Even the "foam-fleece" was "cobbled". Its patterned downiness was beautiful but, mingled with the stinging air and water, it hurt like a hail of stones as it fell.

Stanza 17 returns to the general mêlée before introducing us to the "heroine" of Hopkins's story—exactly midway through the poem. Chaos ensured as the more able-bodied who had climbed up the mastheads were numbed by cold and fell to their deaths whether "to the deck / (Crushed them)" or into the "water (and drowned them)" and those who had simply made their way up from the saloons to the deck were sent by the vessel's careering movement over the side, rolling with the "sea-romp over the wreck". The crying of women and children was heartbreaking: For once the expression is no hyperbole, and Hopkins underlines the fittingness of emotion to reality. This is the scene when the "lioness"—Hopkins's "tall nun"—makes her appearance, "breasting the babble" like some Amazonian warrioress. And indeed spiritual warfare is the order of the day. Hopkins presents her as a "prophetess", as a tower (the prophets of Israel considered themselves "watchtowers" of the people), and as a belfry from which, like a church-bell in the villages of her native Westphalia, men are being called to God.

In stanza 18 Hopkins consults the reaction of his own heart to the nun's intervention. He finds to his amazement a joy in it: "this glee", and enquires "What can it be, . . . the good you have there of your own?" The triumphs of divine grace in her consecrated virginity and her acceptance, in dire circumstances, of a prophet's role have some affinity with his own situation and task, as a Jesuit preparing for the priesthood in a hostile Britain. Hopkins finds himself moved to tears. He reflects on the mystery of the human heart, encased in its skeletal chamber, "your bower of bone", and capable of refined, spiritual pain, "an exquisite smart", just as the body registers physical pain, large and small. What is it the heart is telling him? At first it is unclear: "Have you! . . . Do you!" He ought to know, since the heart is the "mother" of his being, the matrix of his selfhood. As the prophet Jeremiah had warned (17:9), "the heart is deceitful above all things", in Hopkins's words "unteachably after evil". And yet even after the Fall it retains an ability to respond to "truth". Hopkins asks why he is weeping as much from a happiness that sings within him as from sympathy with others' terrible grief: "such a melting, a madrigal start!" The answer is, a penetration of the ever-renewed joy of divine grace. In the Low Mass of the Tridentine rite, at the prayers of preparation at the foot of the altar, the celebrant says, "I will go to the altar of God", and the server replies, "The God who gives joy to my youth". Hopkins exclaims: "Never-eldering revel and river of youth [!]" But here he must not be misunderstood. It is not that the object of his interest is now really himself, albeit in relation to God, so that the nun's drama during the wreck of the *Deutschland* becomes merely a peg on which to hang and then examine his own (to him, more interesting) emotions. The "good" he has is the good he has "there": namely, in her, in that setting, and not in himself at all.

Appropriately, the rest of the poem, all seventeen stanzas of it, will never lose sight of her (and her sisters). In stanza 19 Hopkins reminds himself and us of the scene. Apparently, the tall nun had stood on a table in the upper salon of the sinking ship and thrust her head out of a skylight into the air. In so doing she exposed herself to new danger from the rush of waters across the deck: Hopkins calls them "hawling", an archaism which, used of the wind, can bear the meaning to "veer" or "swerve" but which he probably used here for its sound associations with "howling" and "brawling".[162] The sea means implacable threat, and it means violence too. The salt-water, "[t]he rash, smart, slogging brine", "blinds" her. But she is not so unseeing that she fails to see the *unum necessarium*, the one thing necessary. In fact, she has only one "fetch" in her, a seafaring term for a boat's direction. However disoriented the *Deutschland* had been in its course, however impotent its crew now are to move the ship in any direction at all, the tall nun steers her craft straight as a die. As she "rears" herself up, it is not principally to reach the air but the ear—the "divine Ears", first and foremost, but also human ears, those of her fellow-sufferers, the "men in the tops and the tackle", who heard her even above the noise of the storm.

Hopkins now pauses in his tracks for a moment to consider the nuns' background and its implications. There were

[162] D. McChesney, *A Hopkins Commentary*, 44.

five sisters in all, and Hopkins thought, wrongly, that the tall one whose cry to God the journalists had picked up from the survivors was their religious superior. Hopkins gets no further with their story before he is overcome by the pity of it. Hence the exclamation, contained by parentheses, that occupies all the rest of this verse. The vessel's name, *Deutschland,* was twice "desperate" since it was also the name of the civil society—Germany—which, through its state power, had sent the nuns to an exile that, in the ship named for the country, had brought about their deaths. Hopkins was writing before the naval race between England and the newly unified Germany had started. Before 1870 there was no Germany to be a rival of Britain's. No anti-German feeling, then, should be read into his remark And indeed he at once universalises his comments in the words "O world wide of its good!" Germany has no monopoly on malice. The point is confirmed by his references to not only Martin Luther but also St Gertrude of Helfta (died 1302). Luther was a son of the Thuringian town of Eisleben. Gertrude's birthplace is controverted, but the vicinity of Eisleben is at any rate a definite possibility. To Hopkins Luther was a "beast of the waste wood", both in his boorish personality and low rhetoric and in his destructive effect on the late medieval Church and the unity of Western Christendom at large. Generally speaking, even theologically educated English Christians, be they Catholic or Anglican, have little or no knowledge of Luther's thought, but it can safely be said that his "new doctrine of salvation",[163] the consequence of the original "spin" he put on the Pauline letters, would be hard to reconcile with the *Brautmystik,* or "nuptial

---

[163] *"Die neue Heilslehre"* is the title under which the premier German Catholic theological encylopaedia discusses Luther's doctrinal thought: see J. Höfer—K. Rahner (eds.), *Lexikon für Theologie und Kirche* 6 (Freiburg 1961; 1986), cols. 1224–25.

mysticism", of Gertrude, a Benedictine (or, conceivably, Cistercian) nun and visionary whose "Revelations", otherwise called *The Herald of God's Loving Kindness*, anticipate the devotion to the humanity of Jesus under the title "the Sacred Heart" in which the Society of Jesus came to specialise. (In sharp contrast, Luther's Christology is almost Monophysite in character.) By coincidence, the Latin edition of Gertrude's *Revelations* was published at Poitiers by the Benedictines of Solesmes in the very year of the wreck (and the poem): 1875.[164] But these two strongly differentiated figures, the pious nun and the rebellious ex-friar, are "two of a town". Hopkins compares them to the brothers Cain, the first murderer (Luther), and Abel, the aboriginal "just man" (Gertrude, "Christ's lily'). The two brothers "sucked the same . . . breasts", just as Gertrude and Luther were nourished at the same German hearth and home.

Hopkins has no desire to soften the accusation of anti-Catholicism by imputing benign motives to the Prussian authorities. In stanza 21 we are told baldly the nuns were "[l]oathed for a love men knew in them". It was their integral Christianity that made them "[b]anned by the land of their birth". But if the "Rhine"—the river that waters the Westphalian countryside from where the sisters came—had "refused" them, the "Thames"—the river that flows through the British capital—went one better or, rather, worse. It "would ruin them". Hopkins will shortly show, however, how limited was the ruin the waters of the river estuary could work.

A comparison now follows which is as elaborate as it is forceful and moving. For the ancients *the* hunter par excel-

---

164 *Revelationes Gertrudianae et Mechtildianae* (Poitiers 1875). An improved edition with French translation, under the auspices of the series *Sources Chrétiennes*, superseded this in the later 1960s and 70s.

lence was Orion of Boeotia, a giant who, after his sufferings and death, was placed among the stars, where he appears girdled with sword and club. The stellar constellation named after him sets at the beginning of November when, in the Mediterranean world, storms and rain are frequent. Hence the Roman poets often hailed him as *imbrifer, nimbosus, aquosus,* the showery, cloudy, watery one. Hopkins treats the elements—"surf, snow, river and earth"—as hunting-dogs of Orion, that would "gnash" the sisters in this hour of trial for their faith. But another who has suffered and been exalted, the *Christus passus,* the true Orion, the "Orion of light", is "above", and this storm is his most delicate instrument for testing his chosen beloved. His "unchancelling poising palms" were "weighing" the sisters' "worth". He, the King of martyrs or "martyr-master", had brought them from the sanctuary and choir-stall, the "chancel" of their conventual chapel, for this public testing and witness. Of course, for one to be acknowledged a martyr the Church must find that one died through testifying to a truth of faith or morals. The Franciscans on the *Deutschland* did no such thing. But the tall nun, whom Hopkins treats as their representative, died confessing her faith nonetheless, and the poet regards them, then, as auxiliaries to the *martyrum candidatus exercitus,* the "white-robed army of martyrs". Christ-Orion looks down at them and finds the falling snowflakes a shower of flowers from heaven. In MacKenzie's excellent comment:

> God's lily-coloured curling snowflakes scattered over the Deutschland carried as on inscribed scrolls His testimony to their unblemished service.[165]

So "[s]torm flakes were scroll-leaved flowers, lily showers—sweet heaven was astrew in them".

---

[165] N. H. MacKenzie, *A Reader's Guide to Gerard Manley Hopkins,* 44.

So far we have not heard much of the significance, if any, of the nuns' Franciscanism. Now, with stanza 22, the topic emerges properly for the first time. The approach to it comes via, of all things, the number five. Hopkins had a powerful, in the widest sense sacramental, imagination. As with many medievals, the number five—as there were five Franciscans on the *Deutschland*—immediately suggested to him the wounds of the Lord. Devotion to the Five Wounds of Christ was prominent in late medieval piety, not least in England (the Pilgrimage of Grace, launched to protest the religious changes of Henry VIII's reign, bore the Five Wounds on their banners). In lightly coded fashion, "five" spoke of Christ, as in, for example, the cinquefoil windows of churches or five-porched entrances to cathedrals or shrines. It was his "finding", a means to identify him in such contexts, and his "cipher", his heraldic device as on the banners of the Henrician pilgrims. It could also be called his "sake", a term which Hopkins frequently used in a sense all his own for what in his letters he explained as "the being a thing has outside itself . . . that in the thing by virtue of which especially it has this being abroad".[166] Hopkins's fellow Jesuit, the twentieth-century theologian Karl Rahner, would call that being "symbolic" in the most realistic sense of that term.[167] In the case of the Five Wounds of the Lord, they are, in the historical moment when they were inflicted, a "mark . . . of man's make". But the "word" for that mark, the intelligible meaning it possesses in the divine redemptive

---

[166] *Letters,* 83.

[167] See with an application to Christology, Hopkins's own central concern here, J. H. Wong, *Logos—Symbol in the Christology of Karl Rahner* (Rome 1984). Indeed, this study claims that while Rahner's theory of the "real symbol" has wider philosophical presuppositions and consequences, it originates from his Christology, notably through reflection on the Ignatian Exercises and the devotion to the Sacred Heart.

economy, is "Sacrificed". And, so understood, it is the mark the "martyr-master" personally "scores it in scarlet . . . on his own bespoken", the souls that are dearest and nearest to him, who walk the same way he walked. "Before-time-taken", in the predetermining counsels of God, for Logos incarnate was, by divine foreknowledge, always intended to be the Lamb that was slain, this "cinquefoil token" is not only Christ's "signal", which might imply something external to him or merely conventional in its indicating him. It is also his "stigma", the characterising bloody sign inscribed in his own flesh. Red roses—the "ruddying of the rose-flake"—are flowers suited for the feasts of martyrs. Like a farmer riddling his sheep to mark them out from those that belong to strangers, Christ is found "lettering" with scarlet the fleece of his lambs.

St Paul had spoken metaphorically of the *stigmata* of Jesus carried around in the apostle's own body (Galatians 6:17). But the first time, so far as is known, the "stigmata" became enacted metaphor, physically affecting the body by way of reproducing the Five Wounds was in the most Christ-like saint of Church history, Francis of Assisi: the spiritual "father" of the exiled nuns. Hence Hopkins's outburst: "Joy fall to thee, father Francis", which opens stanza 23. Joy at the victory in, through, and over suffering which will soon be that of his daughters; joy also for the stigmata he bore and what they signified. St Francis had endured and enjoyed a perfect configuration to the sacrificial love of the God-man: "the gnarls of the nails in thee, niche of the lance, his / Lovescape crucified". The stigmata were in Francis's case the "seal of the seraph-arrival", the evidence of the authenticity of the saint's vision of a crucified seraph on Mount Alverna, the moment of his transforming identification with the suffering and exalted Lord. Hopkins presents

the nuns, "these thy daughters", to their heavenly patron: as
a "five-livèd and leavèd" circlet of children worthy of his
"favour and pride". Their seal is not the stigmata but their
deaths, representatively confessing the name of Jesus, in the
"wild waters" of the North Sea. The stanza ends with one of
the most stunning lines in the poem, which verifies what
James Finn Cotter calls Hopkins's intention that "his poems
should explode in the mind and emotions".[168] The sisters
are "sealed" so that they may "bathe in his fall-gold mercies". They pass through seawater now translucent, as in a
seascape by Turner, with divine radiance for those who have
eyes to see what is taking place. Yellow lightning strikes
them in the storm, but it is the liquid "gold" of Christ's saving and deifying grace that falls on them from his Cross. So
it is they "breathe in his all-fire glances", for the true God, as
Hopkins has insisted from the start of this ode, is terrible as
well as wonderful. He is terrible in this storm; terrible too in
the momentary face-to-vision that is final judgment. Hopkins had in mind the opening of the Johannine Apocalypse
where St John sees Christ on Patmos "in the midst of the
lampstands one like a son of man", and reports, "his eyes
were like a flame of fire" (Apocalypse 1:13, 14).

By way of heightening our feel for the disaster—only
ambivalently evil though it was, Hopkins compares his situation to theirs. At his beloved St Beuno's he was "[a]way in
the loveable west, / On a pastoral forehead of Wales". It
sounds idyllic—and domestic, for "I was under a roof, I was
at rest". But "they", the nuns, were "the prey of the gales".
Focussing, like the newspaper accounts, on the nuns' so to
speak "spokesperson", Hopkins describes the tall nun calling

---

[168] J. F. Cotter, *Inscape,* 146. Curiously, Cotter thinks this aim better achieved in the sonnets than in "The Wreck of the Deutschland", but possibly he means not so well achieved in the latter
without the help of his book!

out both to the elements and to her fellow sufferers but most of all to the God-man. In the words she chooses—she "Was calling 'O Christ, Christ, come quickly'", she appropriates the cry "May the Lord come", *Maranatha*, that ends the Book of the Apocalypse. In that book, "The Spirit and the Bride say, 'Come'" (22:17). And its author "hears" the Lord reply, "Surely I am coming soon" (22:20a), which emboldens him to echo in conclusion the words of the Bride (and the Spirit): "Amen. Come, Lord Jesus!" (22:20b). This is her "cross" which will lift her into glory. So she "christens her wild-worst / Best", recognising the presence of her Redeemer in the storm that will terminate her life on earth. It is important, though, that her words have been audible, outer words (as those of the Spirit and the Bride presumably were not). The cosmic elements were the means of her transitus so they merit address as material as themselves. More profoundly, the passengers and crew needed to hear her cry, since it is a prophetic admonition for those of them who will die that day, yet are not disposed for eternity, not in any way ready for God.

Her cry forces out of Hopkins an answering exclamation of admiration: "The majesty! [of it]". But he follows up this straightaway with a question: "[W]hat did she mean?" The answer to the question will come in stanza 28, which is the true climax of the poem. Meanwhile the poet places his enquiry in the context and keeping of the second and third Trinitarian persons, through whom all the relation of the Father to men takes its being and form. He seeks inspiration from the Holy Spirit who—appropriately enough—brooded over the chaos waters in the beginning and is the immediate source of all Christian understanding. "Breathe, arch and original Breath." He then turns to the divine Son who was made flesh and died for her as for us. "Breathe, body of

lovely Death." Was it "love" for Jesus Christ, Bridegroom of
the soul as of the Church, that made her cry out then, as the
waters overcame her? If so, remarks Hopkins, coolly, she
hardly resembled Jesus' normative disciples, the Twelve, who,
when the weather got rough on the Sea of Galilee did not at
all relish drowning with their Master but on the contrary
called out to him to save them (Matthew 8:23–27 and paral-
lels). They were "else-minded" with a vengeance. Or, again,
was the point of the nun's cry desire to hasten the awarding
of the "crown" of righteousness (II Timothy 4:8), especially
as the misery she was enduring made the contrast of the
future "comfort" so much more alluring?

Although Hopkins will not elect that explanation for the
cry, he dilates on the truth it contains in a sunburst of glorious nature imagery. Just think of the May time that scatters
the low-lying grey clouds of a winter that outstays its welcome. Hopkins's astronomical knowledge put him in mind
of the cloud formation called "mammato-cumulus", so
named because it gives the impression of drooping udders:
thus the "down-dugged ground-hugged grey". The clouds
whisked away, the "jay-blue heavens" appear, azure as the
blue patch on that bird's plumage. Glistening in spring
showers (Hopkins appears to use "peeled" here to mean
"pooled", a Scottish usage), and bright with contrasting
colours ("pied"), nature is revealed in her "[b]lue-beating
and hoary-glow": a descriptive phrase for atmospheric conditions which, as MacKenzie points out, makes its point as
much by sound as by sense.[169] At night time too in spring,
what loveliness surrounds us, in "belled fire" (Heraclitus,
whom we have seen to be one of Hopkins's favourite
philosophers, thought of the stars as bowls—and hence
bell-shapes—of fire), and the "moth-soft Milky Way", with

---

[169] N. H. MacKenzie, *A Reader's Guide to Gerard Manley Hopkins*, 48.

its *douce* light soft as a moth's wings. The "heaven" that lies beyond the physical heavens exceeds the beauty of the skies infinitely more than do the glories of spring the dull depression of a winter that will not go away. For Scripture calls this "treasure"

> what no eye has seen, nor ear heard, nor the heart of man conceived, what God has prepared for those who love him.
> (I Corinthians 2:9; cf Isaiah 64:4; 65:17)

—a passage Hopkins paraphrases in the closing line of stanza 26.

Stanza 27 opens with a resounding negative to these various possibilities he has just tried out for size: "No, but it was not these". It certainly was not taedium vitae or a sense of the relentless burdens of a demanding religious life and apostolate that made the nun cry out. It was not a cry "Enough!" extracted from someone sick of "[t]ime's tasking", jaded with existence here below and the constant jolting of life's cart. A heart "sodden-with-its-sorrowing"—alas, Hopkins would know that well by the end of his Jesuit career, in his Dublin period—might call out "Let it be over and done with". It seems less plausible when coming from the lips of someone in imminent danger of death in exciting if horrific circumstances—"in wind's burly and beat of endragonèd seas". Even quiet meditation on the Passion of Christ would be a more likely setting for the expression of a desire to have done and be with the Lord.

Stanza 28 gives us the answer we seek, and an amazing one it is. That Hopkins himself finds it so is apparent from the broken, staccato utterance with which he leads up to it. "But how shall I? . . . Reach me a . . . Strike you the sight of it?" Whatever can "it" be? "It" is a faith-intuition of the Lordship of the Christ who through the cosmic elements

and in no other way now comes to take her to himself.
"There then! the Master, / *Ipse,* the only one, Christ, King,
Head". This capitalised Latin persona pronoun *Ipse*—"he
himself"—is, in the distinctive sense lent it by the total context, the climax of "The Wreck of the Deutschland". That
"total context" includes most importantly Hopkins's doctrinal commitments, nuanced as these were by his Scotism, for
which the sacrifice of the Son is God's first thought of the
world. As Hans Urs von Balthasar points out in his essay on
Hopkins as theological aesthetician in *The Glory of the Lord*:

> [I]f the creation of the world is seen in this way, as an impli-
> cation of the decree of the Incarnation, then it follows that
> the cosmos as a whole possesses, either manifestly or secretly,
> a christological form. And it further follows that through all
> the raging of the elements, all the wildernesses of matter, all
> shipwrecks and ruins, Christ can be coming and truly is.[170]

James Finn Cotter notes the particular force of *"Ipse"*: an
unexpected choice, since Hopkins sedulously avoided non-
English words in his poetry. Cotter points out that in the Vul-
gate version of the Colossians hymn—Colossians 1:15–20, a
text inevitably familiar to Hopkins owing to its resonance
with Scotus's teaching:

> the pivotal *ipse* occurs in the middle verse between the two
> parts of the poem where St Paul states that Christ who is
> firstborn of creation, creator of the world, is the very same
> one who is head of the Church, the first to rise from the
> dead, and the redeemer through his reconciling death.[171]

---

170 H. U. von Balthasar, "Hopkins", in *The Glory of the Lord. A Theological Aesthetics. Vol. 3: Studies in Theological Style: Lay Styles* (Edin-
burgh 1986), 383.
171 J. F. Cotter, *Inscape*, 158.

As Creator and Saviour, whose sacrificial signature ran through the whole cosmos even before he himself consummated all things by his own death on the Tree, the God-man can "cure the extremity where he had cast her". He is *called* Lord of the living and the dead (as God, Hopkins has addressed him so in the ode's very first stanza). Well, then, let him "Do, deal, lord it". Be as good, if also as terrible, as his name. And Hopkins, seeking in his own imagination to retrace the form of the nun's ecstasy, bids the Lord Christ "ride, her pride, in his triumph, despatch and have done with his doom there". Once again, his "doom" is his judgment, which, for the nun calling on him through loving faith, can only be everlasting salvation. That is why his "riding" over the elements is "his triumph", the triumph of his grace in her. Hopefully, alerted by her cry, and through the intercession of the sisters, it was true for many others that day as well.

In stanza 29 Hopkins commends the nun's rectitude of heart and singleness of vision which enabled her to interpret the signs of the seemingly ghastly happening before her, around her. It wasn't easy to "[r]ead the unshapeable shock night", but she at least "knew the who and the why". She interpreted the catastrophe, and indeed all things, present and past, by relation to him who is the eternal Word and who establishes the meaning of every event or process: "him that . . . / Heaven and earth are word of, worded by". Like Simon Peter after the resurrection, she was utterly solid in her faith, immoveable in it as the Tarpeian cliff, part of Rome's Saturnian hill, later known as the Capitoline, and immortalised in English literature by Milton in *Paradise Regained*.[172] That is no generalised "faith", but confession of the God-man. In his meditation points on St Peter Hopkins noted:

---

[172] J. Milton, *Paradise Regained*, Book IV, lines 49–50.

'Thou art the Christ the son of the living God—Praise our
Lord in the words of this confession.—There are two
acknowledgements, that our Lord was the Christ and that
he was son of God. The Christ is the chosen and anointed
men, the Son of God is God.[173]

Hopkins further compares the nun to a beacon fire built,
no doubt, on a rocky headland, which, "blown" by the
wind, is fanned into ever more vigorous flame: "a blown
beacon of light".

After the sound and fury of the riding of the true storm-
God through the heavens, stanza 30 subsides into a devotional whisper: "Jesu, heart's light, / Jesu, maid's son".
Hopkins delights in a calendrical coincidence. The night the
Lord took to himself this bridal companion who had aug-
mented his "glory" was the vigil of the Immaculate Conception of the Mother of God, an annual solemnity falling on 8
December. That was the "[f]east of the one woman without
stain". The conception of Mary and its purpose, the conception of Jesus, were necessarily "one-off": not only past
events but unique events at that. And yet there is a singular
congruence that joins the spotless begetting of Blessed Mary
to the passion of the tall nun. In her mind and heart the
nun also bore the Word made flesh, "heard" him and "kept"
him, and finally "uttered [him] outright". The Fathers of the
Latin church, especially St Leo and St Augustine, insist that
the Mother of the Lord conceived the Word spiritually by
faith before she did so physically in her womb.

The nun's sufferings on the battered vessel were the birth-
throes of Christ's coming to be in her in his full Lordship.
That meant "pain" as well as "patience" for her, and she will
be rewarded. But what of the rest of the company? At first
Hopkins feels soteriologically pessimistic on the subject.

[173] *Sermons*, 254.

Unlike the nun, they did not, so far as Hopkins is aware, confess the Lord Jesus Christ. Unlike her too—though, this is more speculative—they had not had recourse before sailing to the sacrament of Confession, the tribunal of God's mercy. His heart begins to "bleed" for the "[c]omfortless unconfessed of them". But then he brings himself up short. How does he know they are lost? Did they not have the voice of the prophetess from her tower, tolling her bell to "startle" them back? Yes, there is theologically well-founded hope for them in the thought of "lovely-felicitous Providence" which so subtly provided in this emergency for their salvational needs. Surely, then, the wreck was really a "harvest", the tempest less truly scattering bodies than gathering the "grain" of souls into God's eternal barn.

All of which elicits Hopkins's admiring wonder. "I admire thee, master of the tides", who sat enthroned over the primeval flood and even now "with His power girds in the oceans of the world",[174] being as he is "the wharf of it and the wall", "[s]tanching [and] quenching" the sea's irresistible flow. These bounding cliffs of the earth's oceans image the limit God sets to the forces of destruction. More basically still, since God is the "Ground of being and granite of it", even what is hostile to human flourishing in this world of endless change has its foundations in his limitless act of being and so is encompassed by his goodness whose outworking is the salvation intended—if not, thanks to free will, always achieved—for men. His sovereignty is no less for the fact that it "bodes", or as we might say "bides its time". For all that, it still "abides".

How can we further characterise the sovereignty of God? Stanza 33 will tell us. First, it is a "mercy that outrides / The all of water", being more capacious than the totality of the

---

[174] D. McChesney, *A Hopkins Commentary*, 49.

world's seas. God's mercy floats on those waters, an everlasting
"ark", unsinkable ship of salvation for the "listener", those
who hearken to his word. More profoundly still, it is a "love
[that] glides / Lower than death and the dark". The Old Testament ark, in the Book of Genesis, belonged with the
covenant with Noah, itself a preparation for the covenants
with Abraham, Moses, and David. But at the centre of the
New Testament is the covenant made in Christ, which fulfils
and super-fulfils all of these. At the heart of the Paschal Mystery, in which the new covenant is made, comes the descent
of Christ into hell: that entry of the Lord on Holy Saturday
into solidarity with human beings at their wits' end in death,
to which the Cross of Good Friday leads and from which the
victory of Easter Sunday takes its rise. Hopkins sees the
descent as the running down of the "vein" of God's love into
that underworld, where, "pent in prison", were not only the
righteous prophets and saints of Israel but mediocre souls too,
the "last-breath-penitent spirits". Hopkins finds this to be the
"uttermost mark" of the *Kenosis*, the self-emptying of God the
Son who, already humbled by assuming our sin-pocked flesh,
and drained of life by his Passion, now sinks down into the
shadow world, the Limbo of our fathers and mothers. But, as
the Roman Canon insists in the *anamnesis* prayer which follows on the Eucharistic consecration, it is from these *inferi*,
from this utterly low point, that the Lord rises. Hopkins hails
him as "[o]ur passion-plungèd giant risen", "[t]he Christ of
the Father compassionate", and he finds him "fetched in the
storm of his strides"—a "fetching" that is at once the transfor-
mation of cosmic matter entailed in the bodily exaltation of
Christ, through the Resurrection and Ascension, to the
Father's right and also the salvation now offered to the souls
on the *Deutschland* as he comes to them over the waters.

In the final stanzas Hopkins continues to concern himself
with Christ's lawful right to the obedience of all human

beings. In stanza 34, with its dazzling imagery, he has principally in mind, one may conjecture, the reclamation of the former Christendom—of which the Evangelical-Lutheran Prussian State, with its Bismarckian will-to-power, was a lost province. Ardently, the poet calls on Christ himself "[n]ow [to] burn", burn with zeal for his own. He apostrophises the Child of Nazareth as one "new born to the world", for Christ, the *Puer aeternus*, is ever new compared with a fallen creation where in all moral essentials there is nothing new under the sun. He confesses the two natures, divine and human, sung by the Fathers and formulated by the councils of the Church: "Double-naturèd name". He gives thanks for Christ's coming down from heaven—he was "heaven-flung", flung by the power of the philanthropy of the Blessed Trinity. The poet lauds Christ's taking our humanity, without intervention of a human father, in Mary's womb: "heart-fleshed, maiden-furled / Miracle-in-Mary-of-flame". He acknowledges the Word's *homoousion*, his being one substance with the Father and the Spirit and the midpoint of their life: "Mid-numberèd he in three of the thunder-throne!" Hopkins asks Christ to come again not in the obscurity of his first advent at Bethlehem, but not in the world-shaking conditions of his final Parousia either. Instead may he come "Kind, but royally reclaiming his own", not like the thunderbolts of Zeus—a "lightning of fire hard-hurled", but as a shower of welcome rain on the land.

"The land" has not yet been further specified, though the "shire" already indicates a concentration on the country that was Hopkins's own. In the last stanza of "The Wreck of the Deutschland" Hopkins turns explicitly to the religious cause closest to his own heart, the re-conversion of England—here, "Britain", for he was in Wales and in love with Wales when he wrote—to the Catholic faith. Neither the ship nor its single most significant passenger, the tall nun, had intended to do more than call in at an English port. But in the Providence of God things had turned out differently. She was "at our door / Drowned, and among our shoals". The failure—not necessarily, however, blame-worthy—of the marine authorities in England to rescue her was in the rationality of the Atonement, where victims bless their tormentors, an added reason to expect her inter-cession now. "Remember us in the roads, the heaven-haven of the reward". But the good Hopkins hopes for from her prayers is an entirely Christocentric one: "Our King back, Oh, upon English souls!" Christ has "easter[ed]" in himself and in the origination of the Church as the firstfruits of transfigured humanity. Let him now "easter" in "us", in the religious, moral, and civic life of "rare-dear Britain". Let him be radiance to our "dimness", indeed a "crimson-cresseted east", a fabulous dawn with clouds incarnadined by the ris-ing sun. Let him illuminate Britain "as his reign rolls", the reign of Christ the King, whose being and action Hopkins now sums up in a herald's proclamation of titles, "Pride, rose, prince, hero of us, high-priest", and, more rapturously still: "Our hearts' charity's hearth's fire, our thoughts' chivalry's throng's Lord". Balthasar comments:

> Christ therefore stands once more in the place of the eternal idea, which shines through the phenomena: but he is idea as living God and living man, as personal majesty, self-sacri-fice, love in mercy condescending and emptying itself. . . . The Christian, who is able to read this picture of the mani-festation of the glory of God knows that here all truth and therefore all beauty lie, that he owes it to himself to surren-der in love to this archetype, because he owes him his being and existence and can therefore only glorify him in an ascent to him in his life and work.[175]

---

[175] H. U. von Balthasar, "Hopkins", 390–91.

So Hopkins is the "Theologian's Poet", insofar as in this way, like Vergil for Dante, he is a guide to God in Christ, and therefore a guide for Christian thought, Christian culture, Christian life.

SELECT BIBLIOGRAPHY

Primary Sources

The Poems of Gerard Manley Hopkins, ed. W. H. Gardner and
N. H. MacKenzie (Oxford 1970, 4th edition, reprinted 1986)
Correspondence of Gerard Manley Hopkins and R. W. Dixon, ed.
C. C. Abbott (London 1956, 2nd edition)
Further Letters of Gerard Manley Hopkins, ed. C. C. Abbott (London 1956, 2nd edition)
The Journals and Papers of G. M. Hopkins, ed. H. House and
G. Storey (London 1959)
The Letters of Gerard Manley Hopkins to Robert Bridges, ed. C. C.
Abbott (London 1955, 2nd edition)
Note-books and Papers of Gerard Manley Hopkins, ed. H. House
(London 1959, 2nd edition)
The Sermons and Devotional Writings of Gerard Manley Hopkins,
ed. C. Devlin, SJ (Oxford 1959)

General Studies

W. H. Gardner, *Gerard Manley Hopkins. A Study of Poetic Idiosyncracy in Relation to Poetic Tradition* (London 1962, 2nd edition)
J. G. Lawler, *Hopkins Re-constructed. Life, Poetry and the Tradition* (New York 1998)
N. M. MacKenzie, *A Reader's Guide to Gerard Manley Hopkins* (London 1981)
R. B. Martin, *Gerard Manley Hopkins. A Very Private Life* (London 1991)
N. White, *Hopkins. A Literary Biography* (London 1992)

• 215

Particular Studies

P. M. Ball, *The Science of Aspects. The Changing Role of Fact in the Work of Coleridge, Ruskin and Hopkins* (London 1971)

T. K. Bender, *Gerard Manley Hopkins: The Classical Background and Critical Reception of his Work* (Baltimore 1966)

R. Boyle, SJ, *Metaphor in Hopkins* (Chapel Hill, North Carolina, 1961)

J. F. Cotter, *Inscape: the Christology and Poetry of Gerard·Manley Hopkins* (Pittsburgh 1972)

J. Milroy, *The Language of Gerard Manley Hopkins* (London 1977)

W. A. M. Peters, SJ, *Gerard Manley Hopkins. A Critical Essay towards the Understanding of His Poetry* (Oxford 1948; 1971)

A. Thomas, SJ, *Hopkins the Jesuit: The Years of Training* (London 1969)

R. K. B. Thornton (ed.), *All My Eyes See. The Visual World of Gerard Manley Hopkins* (Sunderland 1975)

T. Zaniello, *Hopkins in the Age of Darwin* (Iowa City 1998)

Note

For readers desirous of yet more, in addition to T. Dunne, *Gerard Manley Hopkins. A Comprehensive Bibliography* (Oxford 1976), which in effect is complete to 1970, the Hopkins Society of London publishes an annual update in *The Hopkins Research Bulletin*.